The Customer Centric Sales Process

Aligning Sales to the Buyer's Journey

Jeff Nguyen

Contents

Introduction

The advent of the internet and rise of self-service online research has dramatically shifted control in the buyer's journey from sales teams to the customers themselves. As a result, traditional sales tactics focused solely on promoting products, pricing and generic relationships are no longer effective. Sales organizations that fail to adapt more customer-centric strategies risk losing relevance in the modern market.

Across industries, buyers are handling more of the purchasing process independently through digital channels. According to Forrester research, between 70-90% of the buyer's journey now occurs without any engagement with a sales rep. Armed with product information available 24/7 online, today's buyers often know just as much or more about solutions than the average salesperson early in the evaluation process.

As buyers enjoy more transparency and choice, the motivation for them to interact with potentially biased sales reps continues declining. These empowered customers have high expectations for personalized experiences too. Facing such a starkly different landscape, sales teams stuck reacting with traditional product pitches or waiting for inquiries struggle with irrelevance, declining conversion rates and talent retention challenges in the digital age.

Sales leaders must rethink processes in this customer-first environment. Strategies solely focused on short-term transactions do not resonate with modern buyers looking for trusted advisors invested in a long-term partnership. Instead, forward-thinking sales organizations develop organized playbooks intentionally designed to provide value during each stage of the self-directed buyer's journey.

While buyers determine their own journey, sales teams still have significant opportunities to nurture and guide them toward decisions through helpful interactions such as:

Awareness Stage: Publishing educational blogs, guides and tools to establish domain expertise buyers seek when defining initial needs and problems

Consideration Stage: Providing tailored content like case studies and comparison materials so your brand stands out as buyers assess options

Purchase Stage: Offering consultative guidance, risk reduction data and support resources as part of the proposal process to solidify status as a trusted partner

Successful sales teams recognize they must adapt to changing buyer preferences in order to remain influential partners over the long term. Where marketing used to drive initial interest, today customers research solutions independently online before ever engaging vendors. By aligning sales processes closely with how buyers currently purchase, organizations can regain guidance opportunities at pivotal experimentation stages.

However, maintaining relevance requires more than just closing deals. Forward-thinking sales teams understand the true work of nurturing lasting relationships begins after the initial sale. These representatives view each new customer not as a one-time transaction, but rather the start of an ongoing partnership.

To cultivate strong, long-lasting partnerships, sales representatives should engage customers at least on a quarterly basis. Through review meetings, they assess how needs may be evolving in light of shifting business priorities, market changes, or technical advancements. Rather than taking a reactive stance, sales must proactively addresses emerging requirements to maximize continued value.

Sales can also cultivate communities around educational content and user experiences. Automated content journeys introduce customers to new solutions, capabilities, and industry best practices on an ongoing basis. This establishes the vendor as a trusted advisor constantly helping clients achieve more.

Relationship managers can also actively seek customer references and introductions to expand social evidence over time. Glowing testimonials and warm introductions give future prospects confidence in the vendor's ability to satisfy others in similar situations. This builds momentum that attracts growing volumes as credibility rises.

By focusing sales engagement on lasting partnerships instead of fleeting transactions, organizations fortify influence in guiding ever-changing buyer preferences. Those who maintain relevance through proactive support reap the greatest rewards of expanded markets and growing wallet share with highly satisfied clients. This strategic approach ensures sales maintains influence throughout each customer's journey.

The accelerating digitization of the buyer's journey requires sales teams adapt more consultative, customer-centric strategies based on education and advice versus product-pushing. Although this transition can feel uncomfortable initially, organizations that realign their processes to map seamlessly to how modern buyers want to purchase today will sustain relevance and results. Looking ahead, the human, emotional elements of buying will still crave empathetic sales interactions despite efficiency gains from technology. Therefore, the future sales professionals who blend digital scalability with relationship building are poised to excel.

Chapter One

Sales and Customer Centricity

S elling approaches have transformed dramatically from the days when sales-people pushed products on customers based on one-sided batch pitches. Today's buyers expect and demand a more personalized, consultative journey focused on their unique needs. As a result, customer-centricity now sits at the heart of modern sales strategies within leading organizations.

Traditional product-centric selling is characterized by batch sales presentations focused on promoting features and pressuring customers into deals. While this approach still resonates in some markets, most customers view it as spammy, self-serving and lacking understanding of their actual needs.

Additionally, with 24/7 access to online product comparisons, buyers no longer depend on sales reps purely for information. These limitations make prod-uct-pushing tactics feel dated. Most buyers lack patience for them, decreasing sales productivity and pipeline growth.

Customer-centric selling flips the script by prioritizing buyer needs, pain points and desired outcomes above all else. Sales conversations focus on uncovering the customer's true situation, challenges, priorities and definition of value.

With this understanding, sales teams can tailor proposals featuring the specific solutions, resources and capabilities matching what that particular buyer actually cares about. Instead of promoting generic features, customer-centric sellers position themselves as partners invested in the buyer's success.

As sales continues evolving into a customer-focused profession rather than product-pushing occupation, leaders must invest in capabilities matching modern buying expectations. While certain complex sales still require some feature education, empathy, relevance and assistance now drive most everyday sales conversations. Moving forward, blending digital efficiency with human judgment is imperative to deliver the ideal balance of automation and personalization demanded in the 21st century sales environment.

What it Means to be Customer Centric

Organizations that embed customer centricity into their cultures position themselves to continuously add value in the face of uncertainty. Businesses that fail to deeply understand and deliver on evolving consumer needs open themselves to disruption.

Recent years brought massive increases in new business formations and startups seeking to compete in established markets, with 2021 seeing over 5 million applications versus an average of 400,000 per year from 2010-2019. While COVID-era shifts like remote work and supply chain fragility enabled some formations, this exponential growth underscores the increasing pace of change and sources of potential disruption companies now face.

In particular, digitization dramatically lowered barriers for new entrants to identify consumer pain points and launch solutions addressing unmet needs faster than ever before. Combined with readily available online reviews and comparisons, this empowers buyers to easily change allegiances when they feel underserved.

Facing endless possibilities for disruption, smart businesses pivot from reactive or complacent mentalities relying on legacy successes to proactive innovation focused on continuously exceeding buyer expectations in both current and emerging areas.

This includes conducting journey mapping exercises highlighting gaps where customers feel friction and envisioning the ideal future experience. It also requires empowering teams at all levels to ideate solutions addressing evolving needs instead of decisions flowing only from the top-down.

However, innovation means nothing unless grounded in a genuine understanding of your customers and their contexts derived from direct feedback and insights.

Truly customer-centric organizations obsess over building empathy and trust with buyers through advisory conversations, co-creative project approaches and accountability for delivering promised value. They explore emergent consumption models and market trends shaping future behavior.

This unyielding focus on knowing and supporting customers as individuals, not homogeneous groups, generates endless inspiration for staying relevant.

Installing the above mindsets and practices requires leaders consciously nurturing a culture centered around customer advocacy.

From embedding customer metrics into goal-setting and job expectations to soliciting real-time feedback across the buyer journey, they reinforce behaviors keeping external consumers top of mind. This includes extensive employee engagement surveying to ensure internal customers also feel heard and empowered.

Leaders signal through hiring, training and modeling desired actions that customers sit at the core of all initiatives. Over time, this cultural foundation drives proactive innovation addressing buyer needs today and tomorrow.

What is Customer Centric Selling?

At its core, customer centric selling involves consistently putting the buyer's interests first when it comes to messaging, interactions and solution development.
This includes asking discovery questions to deeply understand their unique
priorities, challenges and definitions of value.

With this context, sellers can tailor proposals specifically addressing the customer's pain points rather than promoting generic product features. When
buyers feel understood and sellers clearly communicate how they can help
achieve desired outcomes, relevance and conversion rates rise.

Taking a Consultative Approach

Consultative sellers build trust and confidence by sharing their expertise. They
provide helpful resources like implementation plans, ways to measure success,
and models to evaluate costs and benefits. This advice allows buyers to make
well-informed choices on their own terms.

The goal is ensuring customers feel confident in their ability to get true value
from any solution. Sellers act as advisors committed to the buyer's ultimate
satisfaction, not just making a transaction.

Examples like proposing a strategy for rolling out a new service shows how
it can be effectively operationalized. Helping craft ways to track important
metrics demonstrates commitment to future success. Guiding interpretation of
financial analyses maintains the customer's comfort in decisions.

By taking a consultative stance, sellers guide buyers to the optimal choice
through education, not sales tactics. Customers thus feel empowered partners,
not subjected to pressure - keeping the seller top of mind as needs evolve. This
earns lifelong loyalty through valued guidance.

Building Relationships and Trust

While a consultative approach starts strong relationships, the best salespeople consciously maintain them long-term. Rather than one-time transactions, these professionals view clients as ongoing partnerships.

Through regular check-ins, renewal consultations, and continuous learning opportunities, top performers deepen relationships over months and years. Their priority remains the customer's evolving needs above all else.

Just as importantly, they develop genuine rapport on a personal level first and foremost. Salespeople remember life details that build real, emotional connections with clients as individuals. Deals come second to these caring bonds of trust.

As a result, clients happily refer new prospects and remain loyal, even if an immediate purchase falls through. They feel confidence in the seller's sincere desire to provide value, not just make sales.

In contrast, transactional sellers rarely cement this degree of reliability and goodwill. Prioritizing people over profits is what wins referrals for life through unbreakable trust in a representative's exceptional character beyond credentials alone. These are the foundations for continually expanded partnerships over the long haul.

As buying power shifts dramatically to customers in the digital age, selling effectively increasingly means selling with empathy, patience and helpfulness. Transitioning teams away from outdated practices to truly customer-centric mentalities takes work but pays dividends. Sales organizations who embrace this buyer-first ethos will sustain relevance in a changing landscape while making the world better through service.

Chapter Two

The Customer Journey

C reating satisfying customer experiences requires understanding that individuals interact with organizations across numerous interconnected touchpoints over time. While traditional sales teams often view relationships narrowly through their own limited purview, leading companies achieve superior results by taking a more complete strategic perspective encompassing the entire journey.

Thoughtfully mapping customer journeys reveals where interactions originate from various internal departments and how they compound to shape perceptions. By charting touchpoints from initial brand awareness through long-term loyalty, organizations identify synergies and gaps between sequential processes. Journey mapping also surfaces opportunities to better coordinate separate initiatives into a seamless omnichannel experience customers value.

For sales teams specifically, journey maps contextualize smaller sales cycles within the holistic relationship timeline. Representatives understand most research happens outside direct interactions and influence stems from facilitating the full process, not just closing deals. Journey perspectives help sales recognize evolving needs from pre-purchase through ongoing support. Addressing full journeys nourishes long-lasting partnerships rather than transactional dealings.

Adopting a journey mindset across departments fosters collaborative efforts enhancing experiences at each stage. Companies satisfying customers through well-orchestrated journeys gain loyal, profitable relationships over competitors neglecting omnichannel coordination. Taking proactive, strategic ownership of entire customer lifetimes drives value through satisfying, effortless experiences.

Marketing: Promotional alignment and lead qualification practices

Service: Implementation and adoption performance

Support: Timely issue resolution and satisfaction benchmarking

Finance: Billing transparency and payment flexibility

This cross-functional perspective illuminates the full picture of dynamic customer needs as well as friction points hampering experiences.

Key Stages of the Customer Journey

The customer journey is the complete end-to-end experience a customer has with a brand over time, across multiple touchpoints and channels. This journey typically progresses through several phases, each marked by shifting needs, questions and priorities that require tailored messaging and interactions. Clearly mapping the customer journey is crucial for aligning business operations to anticipate and effectively serve customers at every stage. While no two buyers follow identical trajectories, most journeys contain similar waypoints that inform an optimized path to purchase and lasting loyalty beyond.

The 5 stages of the Customer Journey are:

1. **Awareness** - Customers first become aware of a brand and its products as potential solutions to their needs. They search for information

online and gather initial impressions.

2. **Consideration** - Customers evaluate a brand and its products as options, comparing them to alternatives to determine if they can deliver on promises.

3. **Purchase** - Customers are ready to make a purchase decision, whether to choose the brand or go with a competing option.

4. **Retention** - After making an initial purchase, the focus shifts to retaining the new customer for repeat business rather than losing them to churn.

5. **Advocacy** - Highly satisfied customers organically spread positive word of mouth and refer friends, family and colleagues to the brand.

The Early Stages: Building Awareness and Consideration

The beginning steps of the customer journey focus on discovering solutions to a problem or need and determining which option best fits. The awareness phase marks the initial emergence of a brand onto a potential customer's radar. Triggered by a pain point or desire, target buyers start researching to learn what products or services could potentially solve their issue. As search terms are entered, social media posts reviewed and recommendations sought, some subset of brands working in relevant spaces will attract attention. The goal now is resonance - does the brand quickly register as offering a viable fix or way to achieve goals? Building awareness requires search visibility, intentional media targeting and word-of-mouth diffusion of branded information.

Once a minimum level of awareness exists, buyers advance into the consideration phase where initial impressions get reinforced or reevaluated. Now the questioning becomes more pressing and direct: Does this company understand my specific situation? Can their offering deliver the promised solution? How do they compare against alternative options? Consideration represents a critical juncture where earned trust must overcome buyer skepticism to make a prospect's shortlist.

Succeeding in these early phases relies on content that clearly speaks to customer needs with the right messaging at the right times. Core value propositions should feature prominently across owned media. Social listening uncovers broader trends and discussions that reveal how people frame their problems. Targeted content then educates audiences by directly tying products or services to desired outcomes. Case studies and testimonials provide outside proof while comparisons can seed preferential positions against competitors.

As prospects connect information to personal contexts, considerations coalesce. Now the emphasis shifts from awareness building to nurturing engaged connections that transition interest into action.

Driving Decisions in the Purchase Phase

Active evaluation, vetting and side-by-side comparisons characterize the purchase phase where future customers weigh final decisions. Having established basic solution awareness and initial viability, the sharper questioning begins. Prospects probe into functional capabilities, implementation plans pricing and contract terms. Self-directed research expands across more channels to gather inputs, from product demos and free trials to expert reviews and user feedback.

The purchasing funnel narrows options while deal sizes grow bigger, magnifying the revenue implications of conversions and drop-offs. Now marketing and sales tightly synchronize to anticipate needs, address concerns and guide preferences. Content offers technical documentation, staff profiles, analyst reports, return policies and other decision accelerants. Sales conversations evolve into consultations around personal goals, infrastructure, specialized features and ongoing support.

With trust established and outstanding objections addressed, buyers ultimately pull the trigger to become customers. Yet even after point-of-sale, the customer journey continues evolving across implementation, onboarding and daily utilization.

Sustaining Engagement Through Retention and Loyalty Building

Post purchase is where business relationships and user experiences converge to determine outcomes. Does reality align with expectations, easing transitions onto new platforms or ways of operating? Do implemented products reliably perform and deliver lasting value? Retained customers spend more over time, evangelize brands that satisfy them and demonstrate the true viability of solutions.

Effective customer retention and loyalty requires carefully designed journeys beyond the sale. Engaged customers not only repeat purchase, they expand utilization via upsells, cross-sells and upgraded tiers of service. Ongoing education and community connections encourage participation while proactive outreach addresses concerns before frustration boils over. Surveys, test groups and advisory panels provide continual feedback channels for product enhancements and process refinement. Long after traditional buyer journeys conclude, retained users continue contributing to business success.

The Ultimate Advocates: Promoters Who Recruit Through Referrals

Brand loyalty reaches its pinnacle when delighted customers graduate to become vocal advocates. By receiving outstanding value from engaging company relationships over time, promoters actively refer friends, colleagues and online followers. Advocacy marks the most powerful inflection point across customer journeys - unpaid advertising at scale. This top tier group helps businesses achieve sustainable growth through constant infusion of fresh opportunities while requiring minimal acquisition costs.

Progress to promotion begins by nurturing customers beyond initial purchases with education, community and VIP perks. Seeking referrals signals the trust and satisfaction to convey authentic word-of-mouth influence. Brand response in turn fuels further positive engagement, as advocates become involved in testimonials, case studies and referral programs. Through recognition and rewards, including premium status, advocates stretch lifecycle contribution and value.

By blueprinting how target customers flow through interconnected journey stages, brands can vastly improve conversion, satisfaction and promotion rates. Plotting awareness, consideration, purchase and loyalty waypoints reveals where messaging and experiences currently fall short. Journey analytics in turn inform resources allocation to where investment efficiently progresses customers to next levels. Journeys never truly end if brands continually deliver evolving value to engaged users and vocal advocates. Map then optimize paths based on want people seek, need and share.

Customer Journey Challenges

Mapping journeys illuminates inconsistencies that challenge the status quo. Gaining cross-departmental support requires communicating benefits clearly while addressing anxieties about the transformation process.

Information Silos

Information silos between different departments can significantly hinder effective collaboration between sales and customer success teams. When organizations allow separate teams to hoard customer insights rather than pooling all data together, it prevents teams from developing a comprehensive understanding of the customer experience across all touchpoints.

This can be problematic as it inhibits teams from helping each other achieve their goals. Sales teams may miss opportunities if they lack insights from customer success interactions. Similarly, success teams could have trouble retaining and expanding customer relationships without understanding the full sales process and latest prospects.

Therefore, executives must take steps to directly incentivize collaboration and break down these silos. They should consider compensation structures that reward cooperative efforts like sharing feedback, instead of solely focusing on individual or departmental performance metrics. Additionally, implementing a single customer database that all teams contribute to can facilitate information sharing across the organization.

It is also important to establish clear governance policies around how customer data is accessed, updated, and used. This helps build trust in shared systems and further encourages teams to pool their resources rather than compete or withhold information. The leadership must model cooperative behaviors as well through cross-functional initiatives and regularly shared reports between departments.

Addressing longstanding barriers requires commitment to organizational changes over time. But breaking down information silos is crucial to allow sales and customer success teams to work interdependently with a unified goal of optimizing the overall customer experience through each phase of the buyer journey.

Failing to Implement Findings

Implementing findings is essential but can prove challenging without dedication to follow through. Merely documenting customer journeys provides little benefit unless organizations act upon lessons learned. Leadership must encourage accountability for improving processes and handoffs identified.

Guidelines should be put in place to facilitate implementing recommendations. Teams need to be assigned ownership over specific changes and work towards set deadlines. Progress must then be consistently tracked through status updates to maintain accountability long-term, rather than just initial planning. Where possible, linking compensation to meeting implementation benchmarks can further incentive completion.

Piloting minor adjustments quickly generates momentum for broader transformations. Communicating insights openly across departments fosters shared responsibility over any issues found. Extensive training may also be required to coach personnel through new procedures and change management. Continual customer feedback ensures changes effectively resolve original pain points while preparation for future refinements.

Celebrating milestones internally motivates effort implementing less tangible progress. Visible prioritization and championing of customer experience initiatives from executives helps to encourage embracing necessary changes despite potential resistance. Embracing rigorous change management appropriately supports journey mapping endeavors in evolving the experiences for customers. Taking the additional steps of acting upon findings and overseeing their application keeps organizations committed to continuously refining touchpoints based on insights gained.

Stale Assumptions

Addressing the challenge of stale assumptions requires organizations to remain vigilant and adaptable. Customer needs and preferences are constantly shifting alongside broader market conditions and technological developments. Therefore, journey maps created at a single point in time may quickly become outdated if teams fail to regularly reassess them against reality.

Keeping maps dynamic necessitates conducting follow up research and measuring customer outcomes consistently over time. Comparing newer findings to original mapping insights allows organizations to evaluate whether current understanding remains accurate or whether a refreshed perspective is now prudent. Teams must be open to the possibility that assumptions provisionally deemed valid may no longer hold true as situations evolve in unexpected ways.

Regular reviews of key journey touchpoints against evolving customer and business data help ensure published maps do not become stale representations functioning merely as reference artifacts rather than living strategic guides.

Leadership should establish guidelines requiring routine reexamination and governance around updating mapped journeys as needed. This may involve timelines for recurrent research, metrics for tracking attrition indicators, or processes to trigger refresh sign-offs.

Remaining adaptive necessitates continual verification that mapping assumptions have not fossilized amid changing realities. Proactively catching moments when revising perspectives is important prevents teams from acting upon outdated understandings no longer reflective of new priorities or behaviors. Adopting such review norms reinforces that journey mapping serves as a flexible process for progressively refined empathy, not static conclusions.

Prioritizing Quick Wins

Addressing this challenge requires balancing short-term improvements with more substantial long-term changes. While teams may be tempted to prioritize fast victories that require little effort, superficial fixes often only provide temporary results rather than sustainable transformation.

Rather than singular quick wins, the focus should be on fundamental workflow restructures and cultural shifts identified through journey mapping as most urgently needed. Superficial adjustments may improve surface level perceptions for a short time but fail to resolve underlying causes of pain points or barriers preventing optimal experiences.

Leadership should guide teams in pursuing holistic solutions, even if benefits take longer to fully realize. Realigning ingrained processes and instilling new mindsets among personnel fundamentally alters how the organization serves customers from the core. Such deep changes establish resilience against future disruptions and the ability to continuously progress experiences.

Guidance is needed to avoid shallow reflexes for the easy path, especially under reactive pressure. Sustainable reforms may start with quick pilots but require long-term management reinforcement. Outcomes demonstrate the commitment to long-haul customer-centricity over momentary gains in appearance. Guidance encourages embracing short-term inconvenience for valuable long-term relationships and competitive differentiation.

A balanced perspective avoids superficial "fixes" and sees journey mapping as an ongoing cycle, not isolated overhauls. Guidance on prioritizing depth over speed optimizes sustainable, loyal partnerships grounded in empathy.

Overcoming these hurdles requires strong executive sponsorship, ongoing communication of benefits, incentives for cooperation, and discipline around continuous improvement. Only then can journey mapping maximize long-term client relationships and satisfaction.

Adopting a Continuous Experience Mindset

Fully embracing the customer journey means internalizing ongoing commitments to facilitating progressive experiences that foster loyalty. This level of customer-centricity influences account management in meaningful ways.

Reps conduct annual reviews exploring how client requirements may be evolving. Such proactive discussions strengthen understanding to continuously align offerings. Analyzing consumption patterns also provides actionable insights into areas necessitating improvement or expansion.

Communication practices shift to a lifecycle perspective as well. Milestone messaging celebrates achievements while promoting next steps. It nurtures partnerships throughout each phase rather than losing touch after close.

Adopting a continuous experience mindset reshapes priorities and cross-department norms. Where transactions once dominated, cooperative experience orchestration now directs planning. Joint ownership of the relationship journey motivates seamless coordination.

With a lifecycle lens, processes consider persistent value delivery rather than singular events. Metrics center on relationship metrics rather than isolated deals. Resources support simplistic journeys rather than product promotion alone.

Those making experience-led transformation gain intrinsically loyal, satisfied customers. Their referrals fuel growth through advocacy as partners appreciate consistent, lifespan care rather than fleeting transactions. Centering experiences breeds profound competitive differentiation.

Continuous journey focus allows sales teams to spot negative signals like support requests indicating poor adoption earlier while crystallizing bright points fostering referral potential. This illuminates a wider range of metrics, initiatives and investments for increasing lifetime value.

Ultimately, the customer journey lends critical context for converting one-time buyers into enduring advocates whose prudent guidance steers new prospects to become loyal customers themselves. Modern selling requires embracing experience optimization, not just transaction facilitation. By distinguishing the extended customer journey from the limited buyer's journey, sales leaders can make decisions elevating holistic loyalty and referrals versus isolated conversions. This mentality promises a compounding competitive edge where each delighted customer translates into multiple new high-quality prospects over months and years ahead.

Chapter Three

Mapping the Customer's Journey

U nderstanding how customers interact with your business across the entirety of their relationship lifecycle is essential for delivering positive experiences that foster loyalty. Mapping out the customer journey illuminates key stages and touchpoints to optimize based on buyer needs and preferences. While methodologies abound, most effective journey mapping processes share common components. By plotting awareness through advocacy milestones with intelligence-building empathy, gaps become visible that allow tailored messaging and seamless hand-offs between teams. The result is an orchestrated path that accelerates conversion momentum.

Step 1: Plot the Steps Customers Take as Their Relationship Evolves

Every customer relationship evolves through a progression of phases, from initial brand discovery through post-purchase loyalty building. The customer journey map visualizes this evolution at critical process milestones and touchpoints. Touchpoints represent moments of interaction across channels - website visits, information gathering, email opens etc. Milestones mark meaningful transitions between stages.

For example, common high-level journey stages include:

Awareness - Learning of a company, product category or solution to a problem

Consideration - Evaluating if offerings match needs and comparing competitive options

Decision - Selecting a specific product or vendor

Onboarding - Getting set up with purchased solutions for usage

Implementation - Integrating solutions into business processes and workflows

Adoption - Using solutions actively day-to-day after ramp up

Expansion - Growing usage through upsells, cross-sells and upgraded tiers of service

Extension - Continuing usage over years while voicing satisfaction and preferring options

Every industry and product niche will contain variations on this lifecycle theme. Delineating stages, then overlaying supporting processes and associated touchpoints provides a blueprint for optimization. The goal is mapping an ideal progression where customer needs sync with business capabilities at proper times to facilitate growth.

Step 2: Build Journey Personas Based on Common Attributes

Rarely does a singular path define all customers. Instead multiple iterations emerge based on shared attributes and behaviors. Customer personas group users exhibiting similar journeys for analysis. Trends exposed help guide appropriate content, offers and channel targeting for each segment.

For example, potential personas may include:

Direct Buyers - Researched requirements themselves before purchasing through company reps. Move quickly from consideration to purchase once engaged.

Influenced Buyers - Learned about solutions from trade publications, events or peers first before engaging. Longer to develop preference so focus on building awareness and trust.

Solution Buyers - Have very specific existing issues requiring fixes or improvement. Often reach out with targeted questions around capabilities before sharing business contexts.

Each persona aligns messaging and interactions to better fit distinct audience expectations. Persona clustering also informs measurement plans that quantify effectiveness at various process points.

Step 3: Map Current and Future Journeys with Data-Driven Empathy

Effective journey mapping combines quantitative behavioral data with qualitative insights around emotional elements. Metrics expose volumes and conversions between stages while direct customer inputs reveal pain points and moments of delight. Together the Why becomes clearer behind the What and When.

For example, usage data may show a large drop off in active users two months after purchase. User interviews uncover this coincides with implementation frustrations around specific software features. The journey map then targets onboarding improvements to better support feature adoption before falling engagement.

Approaching mapping through the lens of customer experience also builds organizational empathy. Internal teams better understand buyer challenges, questions and perceptions. Quantified metrics benchmark performance at different touchpoints. Customer commentary spotlights areas of misalignment between expectations and realities. The combination informs action plans to exceed expectations by rectifying journey friction points.

Common mapping methods include:

- Surveys gathering structured feedback on processes, emotions and desired improvements

- Focus groups exploring specific steps and interactions in the journey

- Individual interviews probing customer recall across touchpoints

- Analytics leveraging behavioral data systems to quantify volumes and conversions

- Testing through tools tracking on-site movements and engagement

Analytics inform the baselining of efforts while qualitative data brings the journey to life with compounding detail. Together they produce an actionable model for enhancement evaluations.

Optimize Journeys Through the Lens of Buyer Needs

The ultimate goal of mapping is creating superior customer experiences that promote mutually beneficial relationships. By deconstructing current journeys against idealized processes, improvement opportunities become visible across channels, offers and messaging.

The buyer perspective grounds this transformation work in what matters most - their needs at each stage. Stepping mentally into persona shoes, look for misalignments between content served and knowledge sought. Assess eased transitions across touchpoints versus abrupt experience shifts from lack of coordination. Feel the frustration around snags and delays that degrade confidence.

These insights rebuild sequences with the customer placed front and center. Potential optimization paths include:

- Orchestrating hand-offs for integrated messaging across teams

- Crafting stage-specific content that answers persona questions

- Refining processes around known persona pain points

- Automating personalized follow-ups post-purchase

- Seeking regular feedback once implemented

Optimization also elevates areas of existing strength. Strong positive correlations between campaign exposure and sales ready leads informs budget allocation and related performance incentives. Outsized returns from particular segments signals opportunities doubling down on associated experiences.

Continual refinement relies on customer input, whether passive or participatory. Voice of the customer programs institutionalize feedback channels while journey mapping workshops and focus groups provide immersive learning. Together they connect strategy to served experience amidst continually evolving buyer expectations.

Key Elements Make Customer Journey Mapping Impactful

For mapping projects to catalyze real change, they must deliver actionable strategic direction. Common pitfalls leave organizations lost in overcomplexity or devoid of human truth by solely relying formulas. Avoid information overload and ambiguity through these best practices:

- Executives sponsor efforts to instill accountability and ensure adoption

- Cross-functional mapping builds connections between previous silos

- Focus initially on primary persona priorities to establish clarity

- Quantify insights but also capture emotional commentary

- Map both present realities and desired future states

- Link journey stages to specific metrics for performance tracking

- Develop personas beyond demographics to include psychological traits

- Update analysis yearly as changes reshape interactions

With the proper framing, information sources, and participation, maps provide clear direction on improving end-to-end journeys. They align systems, processes and even internal culture to what customers need at each stage while optimizing toward ultimately loyal relationships. Commitments to continual refinement also builds infrastructure sustaining engagement over long-term evolutions in the market.

Chapter Four

The Buyer's Journey

U nderstanding the customer journey is essential for designing an effective sales strategy that resonates with buyers and meets them where they are. The customer sales journey encompasses the full life cycle of a customer's relationship with your business, from initial awareness of your company all the way through to becoming a loyal brand advocate. Within this journey, customers interact with your brand in many touchpoints across marketing, sales, and service. By mapping out these various touchpoints and the typical progression of a buyer from prospect to customer, you can gain invaluable insight into how to improve engagement, conversion and retention.

The key is identifying the different stages a typical buyer goes through and the questions and concerns that commonly arise at each phase. For example, the early stages when a buyer is evaluating solutions to their problem often involve building awareness and initial consideration of options. Content that explains the problem being solved with simple, straightforward language is crucial here. As prospects narrow options and compare solutions, they need more detailed information on product functionality and how specifically it can address their needs. Compelling yet honest content that avoids overpromising builds credibility and trust. Finally, buyers want reassurance that they are making the right choice before purchasing, making customer testimonials and free trials valuable later in the journey.

By mapping content, sales conversations and overall messaging to evolve appropriately across the customer journey, you can provide more relevant, valuable touchpoints to move buyers smoothly towards becoming satisfied customers. Eliminate content that fails to connect with prospect needs or establish your expertise and credibility. Use journey analytics to double down on the campaigns, channels and activities that drive conversions. The ideal outcome puts sales teams in a position to leverage journey data so that outreach, conversations and information align perfectly with what a prospect expects and needs to hear based on their mindset and position within the funnel. The result is an exceptional customer experience that accelerates sales velocity and fosters lasting business relationships.

With an optimized sales process that maps messaging and interactions directly to each transition in the customer journey, you can maximize prospect engagement, qualification rates, deal sizes and customer lifetime value. Synchronizing outreach to individual prospect needs avoids wasted effort while progressing opportunities more rapidly towards closed sales. Understanding where customers struggle also identifies areas needing improvement, whether easing friction during purchase processes or better enabling customer success and advocacy. Ultimately if you can trace every step of how a prospect discovers, evaluates, buys and interacts with your company, you gain invaluable visibility into making their experience outstanding end-to-end.

Customer Journey vs. the Buyer Journey

The customer experience extends well beyond initial sales to encompass the entire relationship lifecycle. While the buyer's journey focuses narrowly on transactions, optimizing ongoing loyalty requires embracing a broader customer journey perspective. This oversees engagement from first impression to advocates driving referrals. Distinguishing these related but ultimately distinct concepts clarifies areas requiring tailored messaging and interactions for relationship growth versus one-time conversions.

The Buyer's Journey Maps Purchasing Decision Stages

The buyer's journey specifically traces how prospects evaluate and select products for an initial purchase. It visualizes the typical sequence of stages leading to a transactional exchange of money for goods or services. This sales-centric framework shapes critical selling processes targeting conversion, but concludes its view at the point of sale hand-off.

Common buyer journey phases include:

Awareness - Realizing an issue exists warranting research on potential solutions
Research - Self-directed investigation of products matching needs
Consideration - Vetting specific options around capabilities, pricing and terms
Evaluation - Engaging sales teams for quotes, demos and service scoping
Selection - Determining the best fit option aligned to buying requirements
Purchase - Signing contracts and paying to finalize the chosen exchange

While sales interacts in awareness, consideration and purchase, customer behavior also shapes research, evaluation and selection - transparent yet important touchpoints. Content and messaging must address each stage's unique informational needs. Sales scripts evolve inquiries to discoveries, negotiations to closures in fluent progression.

Understanding each phase in the buyer's journey optimizes synchronized selling tailored to a customer-led buying journey from start to finish.

The Customer Journey Extends Beyond Transactions

In contrast, the customer journey recognizes that winning initial sales marks merely the starting line for ongoing relationship building. This long-term view evaluates true value realization in outcomes versus outputs. It overlays the full spectrum of experiences across the customer lifecycle, from first impression to loyal brand advocate.

While stages vary between business models, phases in the retention and advocacy phase of the customer journey often include:

Onboarding - Getting set up to use newly purchased solutions
Adoption - Integrating solutions into workflows through ramped utilization
Expansion - Growing usage via upsells, cross-sells and upgraded tiers
Extension - Continuing subscription or purchase rates year-over-year
Loyalty - Exhibiting preferential behaviors and emotional affinity
Advocacy - Proactively referring friends, colleagues and followers

This lifecycle perspective expands the very definitions of customer and success. Value creation flows beyond the initial sale to empower outcomes over time, whether hitting utilization milestones or winning competitive bids through trusted advisor status. Loyalty earns increasing share of wallet as advocates drive referral business.

The customer journey also loops back around to inform future buyer journeys for other audiences. Customer commentary guides roadmaps while testimonials and case studies influence new opportunity deal cycles.

Why is the Buyer Journey Important?

Many companies fail to dedicate real effort towards understanding how prospects discover, evaluate and select new products and services. Too often there are assumptions, guesses and differing perspectives across sales, marketing and leadership teams. Without the hard truths provided by journey analytics, attempts to align reach, messaging and interactions to buyer needs miss the mark.

The risks of a fragmented or inaccurate view of the customer journey are substantial in a marketplace where buyers have endless choice and little patience for poor experiences. Prospects now begin their buying process by independently researching options online, from product details to customer reviews. Their journey is increasingly self-directed, and they expect to find answers easily at every stage, whether learning about solutions for the first time or comparing alternatives. If content cannot connect business challenges to helpful offerings or clearly convey value propositions, brands will struggle to make prospect shortlists or justify higher costs versus competitors.

Once in evaluation mode, today's buyers anticipate readily accessible information on pricing, features, implementation and more before engaging with sales teams. Companies that instead hide details behind gatekeeper sales reps or lengthy inquiry forms will experience high drop-off rates. Later-stage buyers want personalized guidance on finding the right solution for their specific needs, goals and constraints. Brands that only deliver generic demos or rigid options end up overlooked for more consultative competitors. At each touchpoint, tight integration of marketing and sales is now essential to anticipate and gracefully guide customers to the next stage.

Without a true 360-degree view of how target customers flow through their journey, sales and marketing campaigns waste crucial resources. Messages become mistimed and misaligned to the priorities and questions that prospects face at different points in their funnel progression. Exploratory content gets pushed at near sales-ready leads while early stage education and awareness building is neglected. The result is poor qualification rates, lower deal sizes and backward slipping through stages that destroy pipeline health. Mapping the journey reveals exactly where and when to engage for optimal impact.

While no two buyers follow the exact same path, analytics expose common waypoints and milestones that inform optimization. Hard truths uncover where prospects currently struggle so that friction can be reduced through better content, tools and messaging refinement. The ideal journey facilitates ongoing learning that qualified sales interactions at exactly the right times and places to maximize relevancy, conversion and lifetime value. But reaching this level of orchestration and seamless hand-offs between teams requires an accurate picture of how customers are nurtured today. Do the necessary work to benchmark the current journey before creating an ideal future state experience that will accelerate revenue.

Distinctions Shape Strategy

Clarifying differences between the buyer process for conversions and full customer lifecycles provides several strategic benefits. It delineates required messaging and content for each phase. During the buyer's journey, offers must prove credibility, showcase capability fit, and justify costs. In contrast, post-purchase communication educates on implementation, highlights successes, and conveys ongoing service and innovation.

Role clarity also optimizes workflows. Sales and marketing shape buyer journeys through complex orchestration to progress opportunities. But closing deals represents a hand-off to customer success teams better equipped to guide adoption and expansion. Compensation and performance metrics should align behaviors to desired outcomes based on growth stage.

Finally, analyzing metrics specific to each journey monitors health. Buyer nurturing evaluates lead quality and conversions rates. But the customer journey examines retention figures, support case impacts, and satisfaction scores as indicators of experience. Holistic dashboarding informs targeted improvements for better alignment.

By distinguishing between the transactional buyer experience and long-term customer relationships beyond initial sales, organizations can better calibrate messaging, measurements and team accountabilities to actual audience needs. This drives sales velocity and conversion rates while building enduring loyalty.

Chapter Five

The Customer Centric Sales Process

When designing an effective sales process in today's buyer-driven world, sales leaders need to take a customer-centric approach that maps each stage of the process to the customer's journey. Too often, sales processes are created in an isolated bubble that focuses more on sales stages and quotas rather than how customers actually make purchasing decisions. This misalignment creates friction and erodes trust between buyers and sellers.

To avoid these pitfalls, sales leaders should develop documented processes that are intentionally designed around supporting customers across the major steps in their decision-making process. This journey-based approach ensures that sales interactions align with how modern buyers want to research, evaluate and select solutions today.

Stages of the Buyer's Journey and Your Sales Process

In the modern buyer-driven digital age, outdated linear sales processes no longer work. To be successful, sales leaders need to design customer-centric processes focused on supporting the entire decision-making journey. This prevents misalignments, builds trust and ensures sales interactions map to how contemporary customers want to buy.

The first phase of the customer journey typically involves early education and awareness building as they look to research potential options online and establish basic knowledge of capabilities and vendors. Your sales process should include corresponding education programs aimed at establishing your company and offerings as a thought leader during this early research stage. This may involve published content such as blogs, ebooks and whitepapers that provide valuable insights into industry challenges your customers face while positioning your firm as an innovative force that can deliver real solutions.

The next step in the buyer's journey usually revolves around more formalized research, direct vendor comparisons and initial discovery calls. Your sales process needs to provide consultative discovery practices to align with this, putting the focus on truly uncovering the prospect's goals, constraints, challenges and vision instead of just pushing product pitches. This consultative selling approach based on asking insightful questions demonstrates a sincere motivation to solve problems versus quickly make sales.

Finally, as the buyer gets closer to an actual expansion, switch or renewal decision, they often require significant hand-holding and guidance on next steps, pricing, implementation and more. Your sales process should assign concierge-style support contacts that can provide white-glove assistance tailored to each customer through the final decision and deployment. This end-to-end journey focus ultimately wins more deals.

Importance of Sales Processes

An optimized sales process is critical for companies looking to drive sustainable and scalable growth. Without a clearly defined process that reflects best practices, sales teams lack the necessary foundation and common language to execute consistency. Sales leaders thus need to prioritize creating an effective sales process to set their expanding teams up for success.

At its core, the sales process establishes a guidelines for customer interactions across the entire revenue cycle - from initial lead to post-purchase support. This roadmap empowers sales reps to have structure around priorities while still allowing room to flex based on each buyer's unique needs. Getting this balance right is key. Too much rigidity and reps won't be able to adapt effectively. Too little consistency and organizations struggle to analyze data, identify coaching opportunities and facilitate team expansion.

Optimized sales process allow leaders to more intentionally build hiring profiles for the specific competencies needed at each stage. Rather than just generically seeking "good salespeople," you can recruit for specific strengths whether around lead generation, discovering pain points or presenting solutions. With defined steps and associated core skills, managers can more easily onboard and ramp new team members leveraging process-centered training programs.

Ongoing coaching conversations further utilize the sales process as a mechanism to highlight what exceptional execution looks like at each step and identify potential gaps hampering deal progression. Tied to this, the process provides the performance management framework for setting individual rep expectations, tracking meaningful metrics and determining bonuses or commissions. Without these insights, properly incentivizing and enhancing team member ability is extremely difficult even with the best intentions.

Lastly, customer-centric sales processes extend beyond initial deal closure to include customer success and retention components as well. The most successful companies today realize the importance of guiding customers through implementation and continued expansion post-purchase. Discarding leads after closing deals is no longer acceptable. To build loyalty and trust that drives referrals and renewals, supporting the entire buyer lifecycle is now imperative.

Developing, implementing and refining a sales process to match ever-evolving buyer expectations remains foundational for sales leaders seeking to enable growth. Your unique process acts as the playbook from which hiring, training, coaching and customer success functions either succeed or falter. Prioritizing these best practices ultimately allows organizations to unify customer interactions for sustained sales excellence over the long-term.

Creating an Effective Sales Process

In order to sell effectively at scale while delivering tailored, consultative customer experiences, sales teams require a practical methodology guiding productive interactions across the revenue cycle. This documented process playbook provides the necessary common language enabling consistent execution across large, dispersed teams.

However, far too often organizations fall into the trap of either overly rigid or completely ad-hoc approaches. Either extreme hampers reps' ability to flex to match individual buyer needs. The key lies in striking the right balance. You must shape processes that standardize only truly mission-critical steps while empowering customer-aligned customization at local levels. Constructing this blended methodology requires deep insights into how target personas actually navigate purchasing decisions mixed with real-world sales performance data.

Delving deeply into customer buying stages through journey mapping lays the foundation for continuously refining sales operations. With empirical research guiding refinements, teams can establish optimized processes supporting seamless execution as breadth expands.

Sales, marketing and success teams also collaborate closely to refine touchpoints between stages. Joint evidence-based reviews identify where adjustments fortify transitions or handoffs for evolving buyer personas.

Understanding Buyer Needs

The first step in outlining an optimized sales process is diving deep on your target buyer persona to intimately understand their priorities, pain points, and decision-making journeys. Where are they coming from? What problems do they face? How do they normally seek to resolve those challenges? Building empathetic knowledge of your ideal customer provides the foundation for constructing a tailored process to guide them to solutions.

Mapping the Buyer's Journey

Once you have researched your buyer persona, the next phase involves mapping their typical journey from initial problem awareness all the way through to eventually purchasing and implementing the right solution. Chart out the logical progression of steps persona groups usually take including critical decision points, roadblocks, and areas where they need vendor assistance to move forward. The more insights generated around how audiences actually buy, the better equipped you will be to align sales interactions.

Defining Process Steps

With a clear picture of the target buyer journey, sales leaders need to define the required process steps that enable sales reps to actively progress qualified, strong-fit opportunities through each buying phase. These steps should focus reps on understanding needs, communicating value, navigating decisions, and supporting adoption. Defined stages must also include exit criteria specifying exactly what buyer outcomes and sales actions are required to advance deals. For example, what demonstrated buyer commitment or quantified results are needed before proposing solutions?

Streamlining and Optimizing

It is important not to overwhelm sales teams with an overly complex process full of extraneous steps. The goal is to streamline guidance around the truly critical, high-impact actions that need to occur in every customer interaction to drive deals forward and cultivate loyalty. Sales methodology should ultimately facilitate customer success while also setting up the organization for efficient scaling and excellence. Frequently refine processes based on real-world performance data, buyer feedback and team input to keep it current.

Embracing a Customer-First Sales Mindset

The foundation of customer-centric selling is prioritizing understanding over pushing products. Rather than defaulting to pre-packaged capability pitches, truly consultative sellers adapt each interaction based on the individual buyer's specific situation. This empathetic approach focused on listening first and proposing solutions second demonstrates authentic commitment to solving problems versus quickly making sales.

Ask Relevant Questions Before Offering Opinions

With today's abundance of independent information sources, buyers no longer need sellers telling them what they should think. Customer-centric reps instead drive value by asking insightful questions uncovering the prospect's unique motivations, constraints, and vision. It's about guiding stakeholders to think differently about challenges and opportunities versus convincing them your solution is best.

Promote Product Usage, Not Just Features

Rather than emphasizing generic capabilities, best-in-class sellers demonstrate how their offerings practically alleviate pain points within the customer's daily work. Walk prospects through real-world usage scenarios highlighting how adopting your solution would tangibly improve their organization's operations and outcomes. This practical approach keeps conversations focused on addressing job-to-be-done.

Target Decision-Makers, Not Just Users

While individual usage insights are still vital, customer-centric sales requires prioritizing the people controlling budgets. Sellers need to guide stakeholders with authority to invest in change towards recognizing why overcoming status quo constraints with new solutions aligns to strategic goals. User wish lists are secondary to executive mandates.

Empower Buyers to Progress on Their Timelines

With long sales cycles the norm, sellers striving to be consultative partners cannot afford impatient attitudes. Let the buyer's readiness dictate next steps, not arbitrary internal forecasts. Customer-centricity means accepting purchasing decisions as a journey rather than a single event. Give stakeholders room to build consensus naturally even if it challenges predictability.

Simply put, the Customer-First Sales puts emphasis on having a conversation with the customer, not a presentation.

Chapter Six

The Customer Centric 7 Step Sales Process

In an increasingly competitive business landscape, sales organizations can no longer rely on outdated linear processes mismatched with how contemporary customers actually make purchasing decisions today. To drive sustainable growth through relevant, consultative interactions, sales leaders need to architect methodology directly shaped by target buyer journeys.

The essence of designing truly customer-centric sales processes centers on deeply understanding both buyer and seller milestones through each opportunity stage while optimizing activities to guide aligned mutual progress. By balancing prescriptive steps ensuring consistency amidst customization, sales teams gain the dual benefits of standardized best practices and situational adaptation skillsets to facilitate deals effectively.

Core to this journey-focused approach is elaborating clear objectives, activities and outcomes creating visibility for both parties into what success looks like at each point - building transparency and trust. When structured intentionally around supporting customers across the major steps in their decision-making, sales processes become powerful assets accelerating growth.

The 7 steps provide a clear process for salespeople to follow. It gives them guidelines while still allowing flexibility based on each customer's unique needs.

Stage 1: Qualification

Traditionally in the qualification stage, the sales rep focuses on gathering information to determine if the potential customer is a good fit from a business and financial standpoint. They ask questions about needs, budget, timeline, and decision process. If the opportunity meets certain criteria, it is moved to the next stage.

A more customer-centric approach to qualification shifts the focus to understanding the customer's unique goals and challenges from their perspective. Rather than just assessing fit against preset criteria, the rep seeks to understand the customer's specific pain points and priorities through open-ended conversation. By deeply listening and questioning to gather insights, the rep can better determine how to create value instead of just qualifying deals. This consultation helps establish trust and positions the rep as a solution partner rather than just an information gatherer.

Buyer Objectives

During the qualification phase, target buyers are typically in the early stages of exploring potential solutions to business problems they've identified but not yet fully quantified or prioritized solving. Their focus revolves around passive research to establish basic solution awareness and initial vendor considerations to gauge the art of the possible. Buyers aim to determine whether investing in further exploration of needs and options appears warranted given other initiatives already underway.

Seller Objectives

The seller's priority must center on guiding qualified target accounts from basic awareness into active confirmed opportunities driving towards a buying decision. This requires an inbound methodology attracting persona-aligned targets then confirming qualification criteria through discovery conversations uncovering budget, authority, need and timeline. Sellers must gain enough initial insights to determine investing additional pursuit resources makes strategic sense while giving buyers a vision of possibilities.

Common Activities

During qualification, buyers commonly conduct light market scans through web research, peer inquiries and initial vendor outreach calls to gather basic capabilities overviews. Sellers often attract target accounts through thought leadership content addressing common persona pain points then utilize sales inquiries and discovery calls to confirm buyer profiles.

Verifiable Outcomes

To progress promising leads from qualification to the needs and solutions exploration phases, certain verifiable outcomes need to occur aligned to core BANT criteria:

Budget - Confidence budget exists either immediately or longer term
Authority - Identify key decision makers/champions that can build consensus
Need - Quantify current state gaps/pains tied to strategic goals
Timeline - Define buying vision/roadmap even if flexible

Additionally, the buyer and seller should agree proper potential exists and joint exploration appears mutually worthwhile based on capabilities matching initial requirements. Both sides must be compelled to invest more time progressing the opportunity.

Stage 2: Preparation

Traditionally in the preparation stage, the sales rep focuses on learning their own company's product capabilities and formulating a proposal tailored to the perceived needs discussed in qualification. The goal is to control the conversation and position their own solution.

A more customer-centric approach has the rep gain a deeper understanding of the customer's desired outcomes before determining the best approach. Rather than immediately focusing on their own offerings, the rep takes time to discuss the customer's current challenges, priorities for the future, and views on success. By listening without bias, various options can be considered in the customer's full business context. This consultation prepares an informed dialogue where the customer makes the choice, based on which path best achieves their strategic goals. The rep acts as a guide empowering the customer instead of simply controlling the direction.

Buyer Objectives

During the preparation phase, buyers work to fully quantify current state gaps versus goals, benchmark peer practices, build consensus on must have capabilities and craft initial visions for solutions pathways tied to strategic priorities. Buyer focus centers on assembling foundational knowledge enabling informed vendor evaluations and solution shaping workshops. Preparation activities drive clarity on objective must haves separate from flexible nice to haves when comparing offerings.

Seller Objectives

On the seller side, effective preparation comes down to deeply understanding target buyer needs beyond surface features to uncover the underlying business goals and use cases driving technology investments. This requires research into industry trends, challenges and peer adoption patterns to better grasp the customer's context. Sellers must internalize personas and buying committees to tailor messaging in vision sharing sessions. The time invested directly correlates to relevancy of guidance provided during evaluation interactions.

Common Activities

Typical buyer preparation steps involve formalizing selection criteria through current state analyses, future vision brainstorming and building cross-functional consensus on prioritization factors across stakeholders. Sellers commonly develop detailed customer profiles researching target account contexts, history and needs while also readying tailored capability presentations, ROI calculators and solution visions addressing likely evaluation elements.

Verifiable Outcomes

For both buyers and sellers, core measurable outcomes marking the end of the preparation stage center on establishing shared vision between all parties on what solution success could look like and agreeing on must have components based on the customer's unique situation. Additionally, buyers should formally define business cases, document key challenges, craft preliminary requirements and prepare for solution shaping working sessions. Sellers need to demonstrate deep knowledge of the customer's environment and craft aligned value proposals.

From preparation comes alignment on a shared view allowing buyers and sellers to efficiently evaluate options against metrics directly tied to the deal specific context. Both sides enter the selection phase armed with artifacts driving productive working sessions.

Stage 3: Approach

Traditionally in the approach stage, the sales rep focuses on convincing the potential customer that their proposed solution is the optimal choice. They highlight product features and competitive comparisons. The goal is to move the customer towards a buying decision on their terms.

A more customer-centric approach has the rep exploring options through the customer's lens during consultative discussion. Rather than pitching one choice, the rep facilitates an interactive dialogue where the customer shares business challenges, performance benchmarks, and cultural fit considerations most crucial to their evaluation. By drawing out customer insights, multiple potential paths are considered impartially. This discussion builds understanding and investment as the customer approaches the next stage empowered with ownership of the decision. The rep acts to inform the customer's journey, not manipulate the destination.

Buyer Objectives

For buyers, the overarching goal of the approach phase centers on determining which subset of identified vendors warrants further evaluation based on technology alignments and domain expertise. To progress opportunities beyond initial explorations, buyers need guidance validating solution requirements and buyer criteria while gaining exposure to differentiated value delivery capabilities from shortlisted providers. The approach sets the foundation for more extensive scoping and demonstrations.

Seller Objectives

Effective sellers leverage the approach to spark active evaluation interest separating themselves from the pack as uniquely qualified to guide the customer's desired business transformation. This requires showcasing intimate knowledge of the prospect's goals, challenges and processes to earn credibility for follow-on working sessions. Sellers must compel stakeholders to devote more time towards quantifying opportunities together.

Common Activities

Buyers commonly undertake reference calls with existing vendor clients and high-level capability briefings to gauge differentiation. Sellers often facilitate tailored capability vision sessions aligned to buyer needs as well as provide access to technical experts and innovation leadership. Both parties openly discuss desired next steps for pilot projects, discovery workshops and solution shaping.

Verifiable Outcomes

For the approach stage to conclude successfully, buyers and sellers should agree in writing to defined next steps progressing the opportunity forward including scheduling workshops, scoping calls, solution demonstrations and bonefide proof of concept testing. This concrete commitment from both sides to devote additional time and resources marks the transition from conversations to concerted evaluation and procurement.

Documented success metrics might encompass formalizing a statement of work for collaborative opportunity quantification, an executed proof of concept trial agreement and mutual closure plan detailing follow-on working session logistics and attendance. Culminating the approach stage comes down to locking in buyer participation advancing evaluation.

Stage 4: Presentation

Traditionally in the presentation stage, the sales rep focuses on showcasing how their proposed solution specifically addresses the customer's needs based on the proposal created earlier. The goal is to gain commitment by winning them over through convincing arguments.

A more customer-centric approach has the rep tailor the presentation based on deep insights into the customer's priorities, as explored previously. Rather than simply promoting a predetermined solution, the rep facilitates discussion around any options that could potentially fulfill strategic objectives. Concerns are addressed through collaborative dialogue, with multiple perspectives respectfully considered. This consultation frames the decision as mutually beneficial long-term partnership based on trust, not short-term purchase based on pressure. The rep ensures all factors most crucial to the customer's success are represented to empower their choice.

Buyer Objectives

For buyers, the presentation phase represents a pivotal milestone placing verified solution options side-by-side to evaluate real-world functionality against documented requirements. Buyers enter presentations seeking validation top vendors can deliver concrete business impact tied to defined use cases and success metrics. The goal is determining who brings the optimal mix of alignment to needs and differentiation to warrant selection.

Seller Objectives

Effective sellers view the presentation as an opportunity to solidify status as the ideal partner well-equipped to guide the customer's desired transformation based on proven expertise and technology capabilities. Presentations should reinforce core value drivers through demonstrations explicitly aligned to the buyer's quantified opportunity, use cases and success metrics. Sellers must compel stakeholders that they offer an uniquely suited solution.

Common Activities

Buyers commonly facilitate scripted solution demonstrations to technology decision makers and user groups focused on marketed functionality and delivery approach. Sellers tend to undertake customer-specific presentations centered on real examples showcasing how the proposed technology enabling desired processes and outcomes given the buyer's constraints. Both parties discuss implementation expectations, change management and measureable results.

Verifiable Outcomes

For presentations to achieve their dual goal of validating or eliminating solutions from consideration, buyers and sellers must leave with clear, documented next steps. Buyers should compile technical capability and viability assessments against original requirements as well as capture key stakeholder feedback. Sellers need to quantify decision driver impacts into financial models tied to mutually agreed metrics.

Beyond eliminating vendors misaligned on capabilities, buyers desire leaving presentations with concrete ROI projections and visibility into realizing the benefits used to justify investments. Likewise, sellers achieve success when the presentation drives buyer approval to progress negotiations exploring contractual deployment options. Both parties gain clearer vision.

Stage 5: Realization

Traditionally in the realization stage, the sales rep focuses on implementing the agreed upon solution and fulfilling the terms of the contract. The goal is to ensure deliverables are provided per the proposal and prevent issues that could derail progress.

A more customer-centric approach has the rep partner with the customer to maximize long-term value realization beyond contractual obligations. By continuously understanding evolving priorities, the rep identifies opportunities for added benefits previously unforeseen. Through respectful consultation, optimizations are made mutually-agreeably versus unilateral decision making. The rep acts as a solution guide over time, not just a transactional vendor, ensuring realized outcomes far exceed original expectations to cement a trusting relationship. Impact is measured collaboratively based on what matters most to the customer's strategic objectives and experience.

Buyer Objectives

For most buyers, selecting a final solution marks only the beginning to a longer implementation journey realizing expected benefits over time. During realization, buyers focus intently on negotiating favorable contractual terms, safeguarding flexibility and orchestrating integrated deployment plans applying user feedback and mitigating disruptions. Maintaining leverage to ensure providers deliver on capabilities claims underpins activities.

Seller Objectives

With deals fully greenlit, sellers shift focus towards expanding scope where possible and initiating services components as trusted advisors. This requires deliberately balancing urgency helping customers kickstart usage while avoiding overwhelming resources. Sellers must guide adaption ensuring sustainability of changes enacted. Realization lays the foundation for lasting partnerships extending beyond initial sales.

Common Activities

Buyers commonly finalize all legal and payment details, communicate rollout plans across the organization, and identify pilot groups to phase more significant changes. Sellers undertake solution configuration, data migration activities and user training while assigning customer success resources to track results. Both parties detail regular governance touchpoints monitoring progress.

Verifiable Outcomes

The core realization milestone marking deal completion encompasses formally executing contracts, integrating technologies and going live to capture quick wins verifying value delivery. Additionally, buyers should observe increased user adoption, process efficiency gains and cost savings against projections. Sellers track usage, satisfaction and expansion metrics to showcase impact.

Realization represents the point where vision gets translated into tangible outcomes. Buyers realize increased capabilities while sellers realize lasting revenue opportunities throughrenewals and add-ons over time.

Stage 6: Perform

Traditionally in the perform stage, the sales rep focuses on ensuring product implementation milestones are met and contract terms are fulfilled. The goal is to avoid penalties for non-performance.

A more customer-centric approach has the rep partnering to maximize long-term value and success beyond contractual obligations. By gaining deep understanding of strategic goals, priorities may shift over the relationship. The rep identifies opportunities to further optimize and grow value through consultation. Continuous learning and adjustments keep the solution tailored to the customer's evolving needs. Impact is measured not by conforming to specific actions, but by collaboratively assessing outcomes most important to the client's experience and priorities. The focus remains a true partnership where success is defined mutually based on trust, versus a transactional vendor relationship.

Buyer Objectives

During the perform phase, buyers focus intently on tracking solution performance against documented targets and adoption levels across end-users to guarantee expected return on investment. Buyers must validate products and services deliver ongoing value tied to original justifications. Monitoring key performance indicators enables course corrections keeping projects on track.

Seller Objectives

With contracts secured, sellers now aim to demonstrate consistent excellence meeting signed service levels and supporting users to ingrain solution stickiness. This requires proactively identifying areas for performance improvements, up-sell opportunities and user community development to nurture loyalty. Sellers must spotlight value frequently.

Common Activities

Buyers commonly facilitate regular business reviews analyzing usage metrics and value realization trajectories against plans to showcase progress to leadership. Sellers undertake quarterly account planning, orchestrate executive sponsorship touchpoints and assign customer success resources to identify quick performance enhancement wins.

Verifiable Outcomes

For the perform stage to fulfill its purpose of cementing solution stickiness, buyers need to realize their desired outcomes based on verified metrics early and often. Whether improved employee productivity, cost savings or revenue gains, showcasing business impact repeatedly is essential to ongoing investments. Sellers achieve success by increasing scope via usage expansion across other groups, executing contract renewals and launching new capability upgrades. Early and consistent value visibility fuels lasting partnerships.

Ultimately, ideal perform phases result in buyers reaching their objectives, improving processes and adopting seller offerings more broadly. Sellers earn trusted advisor status. Both parties progress towards a renewal discussion with history demonstrating a solid return on the original selection decision.

Stage 7: Communication

Traditionally in the communication stage, the sales rep focuses on status updates and tracking deliverables/payments according to the contract. The goal is to ensure contractual obligations are being fulfilled.

A more customer-centric approach has the rep engaging in dialogue to understand evolving needs, gather feedback, and ensure long-term success. Rather than simple status updates, conversations explore value realized, solicit suggestions for improvement, and discuss future plans/challenges. The rep acts as a trusted advisor focused on the customer's growing success more than contractual details. Insights continuously adapt solutions to maximize strategic impact. Both parties mutually commit to the strength of the partnership over time. Communication becomes a two-way knowledge exchange where loyalty stems from outstanding lifetime customer experience and business outcomes.

Buyer Objectives

For buyers, ongoing communication fuels visibility enabling evidence-based evaluations of solution performance and relationship health. Constructive dialogues focused on mutually agreed success metrics and adoption milestones provide valuable insights guiding expansion decisions and partnership invest-ments. Communication alignment to business outcomes is key.

Seller Objectives

Effective sellers realize elevated communication represents a primary lever strengthening account control and loyalty. By maintaining regular visibility into customer health and proactively suggesting improvements, sellers earn rights to shape future buying criteria. Communication puts sellers first in line to address additional needs.

Common Activities

Buyers commonly require usage statistic reviews, milestone tracking reports and account planning presentations as part of standard governance touch-points monitoring progress. Sellers facilitate executive business reviews, adop-tion benchmarking analyses and upcoming roadmap advisory discussions to demonstrate commitment.

Verifiable Outcomes

The core communication stage objective for both buyers and sellers centers on formally reviewing solution performance against documented targets on a recurring basis to validate existing investments and guide potential next steps.

For buyers, reports need to demonstrate clear ROI based on agreed metrics like utilization, service levels and business output gains. Sellers achieve joint success by showcasing client achievements, sharing new innovations and discussing expansion options applying lessons learned.

Open communicationfueling tangible value powers everything from renewal decisions to referrals to upgrade orders. It remains the bedrock of sales excellence before, during and after deals close.

Chapter Seven

Tailoring Your Sales Process to the Buyer's Journey

The starting point for effectively tailoring any sales methodology lies in deeply researching how your specific target buyer personas navigate making purchase decisions today. Where historically linear sales funnels sufficed, modern journeys are increasingly complex involving multiple touchpoints across digital and human channels. Seeking to simplify, contemporary buyers follow common high-level behavioral phases progressing from early research to active evaluation and ultimately transaction.

With detailed visibility into your audience's preferred steps, sales leaders can then intentionally shape documented processes guiding aligned interactions. Common buying phases like Early Research, Comparison and Selection should have corresponding sales stages guiding reps to provide relevant consultation, education and support matched to each mindset. By designing prescribed activities catering to buyer needs in each phase, sales methodologies drive fluid progressions forward based on value delivered rather than arbitrary quotas.

Anchor Your Sales Process on Buyer Actions

At its core, designing a customer-centric sales methodology means architecting a fluid framework tuned to facilitate natural buying journey cadences rather than rigid processes prioritizing seller milestones. This entails mapping required sales activities directly to the actual steps buyers progress through during typical purchasing decisions. The priority shifts from hitting arbitrary quotas to guiding aligned interactions matching broader behavioral momentum.

The key transformation lies in redefining what compels stage movements. Rather than allowing sales reps to unilaterally advance opportunities based on completing generic tasks, progression only occurs when buyers demonstrate incremental commitments revealing they have achieved the required knowledge and consensus to support next steps.

For example, transitioning beyond initial discussions would require the buyer formally documenting feature expectations or participating in diagnostic workshops. The sales rep can help influence the pace but cannot force progression without buyer acts. This approach ensures sales stages align to buying phases.

An ancillary benefit of anchoring stage gates to buyer actions is enabling customer control over setting the cadence aligned to their constraints. Reps cannot arbitrarily speed up or slow down deals. This facilitates optimal timelines for buyers assembling the necessary budget, resources and consensus required before transacting as gaps get addressed through relevant seller supports.

Ultimately, the priority shifts from closing deals fast to cultivating the right buying environments positioning customers to adopt solutions sustaining change over time. This consultative guidance mindset earns trust accelerating sales through insight versus friction.

Additionally, given buyers rarely follow perfectly linear journeys, allowing their demonstrated steps to shape interactions provides clearer visibility for sales reps into true, subsurface commitment levels despite what stakeholders might claim. Genuine interests get revealed through participation. Leaders gain better context for forecasting and alignment.

By mirroring buying journeys, sales processes transform into gauges measuring traction. Deals stagnating at certain points clearly signal barriers requiring resolution before continuing. Mapping phases to actions fosters transparency.

Accelerating Decisions Through Journey Mapping

The starting point for optimizing conversion trajectories lies in researching exactly how target buyer personas navigate from problem awareness to eventual vendor selection today. Sales leaders need visibility into key steps, research sources, selection criteria, and who holds budget authority across current purchasing journeys. These insights spotlight key moments of influence.

Identify Primary Transition Triggers

With detailed process visibility, next focus on identifying the primary triggers compelling transitions from one stage to the next. What actions indicate buyers expanding awareness versus comparing options? How can you accelerate these triggers through aligned messaging and content offers? Perhaps ease of competitive comparisons sways selections.

Construct Dialogues Targeting Each Stage

Equipped with transition triggers, sales and marketing teams can shape targeted dialogues matching persona needs at each junction. Early-stage education addressing common pain points should evolve into insider implementation guidance and leadership envisioning positioning your team as progress partners.

Refine Touchpoints to Needs

Dated one-size-fits-all sales processes fail modern buyers. Sellers now need arsenals of touchpoints—from personalized emails to intent-based chatbots to lifecycle call scripts—tuned to buyer contexts. Meet them where they are with what they need to move forward. The right message at the right time accelerates decisions.

Continuously gather customer feedback and journey analytics to refine conversion playbooks over time as new insights emerge. Evolving buyer behavior models through experience and technology integration sustains competitive differentiation achieving results beyond industry standards.

Core Buying Stages

Despite purchasing variability at individual levels, overarching behavioral patterns help categorize most customers into three macro journey stages including Awareness Building, Consideration & Comparison and Selection Implementation. Grasping differences across each phase equips sales teams to provide relevant support.

During early *Awareness Building*, target researchers commonly assemble basic solution perspectives understanding capabilities in the market today that could alleviate identified pain points for exploration. This phase involves outward bound light vendor inquiries rather than deep internal facing consensus creation so interactions require more flexibility and educational insights versus rigid scripting.

The *Consideration and Comparison stage* shifts focus toward formal requirements shaping, complex data gathering across digital and human sources and initial capability analyses weighing various technology strengths in relation to current and aspirational processes. Sales reps able to demonstrate advisory expertise balancing tactical realities and strategic visions distinguish themselves positioning for contract discussions.

Finally, *Selection Implementation* encompasses a flurry of stakeholder alignments finalizing budgets and terms, executive re-verification of expected ROI against targets and orchestrating nuanced technology configuration ensuring continuity during transitions. This stage demands patient urgency from sellers allowing quick wins while supporting lasting adoptions.

Optimizing the Sales Perspective

With detailed visibility into how target buyers navigate each journey phase, sales leaders gain at scale advantages progressing qualified opportunities by aligning team activities to needs. Certain core competencies take on heightened importance during certain stages.

Early education and insight selling best practices prove most productive when persona groups are expanding solution awareness understanding what is newly possible. Leadership positioning and industry vocabulary prepares the ground for deepen explorations.

As buyers commence comparing solutions against current and desired states, sales teams add crucial value guiding structured capability analyses through detailed requirements definitions, workflow evaluations and future visioning exhaustive in scope yet efficient analyzing tradeoffs.

Finally, during final selection rolling into implementation, reps able to maintain big picture transformations in balance with step-by-step configurations ensure new technologies deploy securing quick adoption wins setting up longer term stickiness for account growth via renewals and expansions over time.

By complementing buying journeys with optimized support matching ever-evolving needs, sales teams facilitate frictionless aligned progressions through each opportunity. They guide the journey.

Chapter Eight

Integrating Customer Insights into Sales Strategies

D efining strategic priorities that map to organizational capabilities and external opportunities is essential for focusing direction and resources towards profitable growth.

However, the process for actually determining those priorities is not always straightforward. It requires thoroughly analyzing massive amounts of data across macro trends, industry landscape, competitor offerings, consumer behaviors, financial performance, operational capabilities, and institutional knowledge and history. With so many complex, interconnected forces at play externally and internally, it is crucial to have a systematic approach for identifying patterns and deriving strategic priorities.

This clear methodology allows you to synthesize the flood of inputs into targeted outputs – the handful of strategic priorities centered on the intersections of organizational strengths, consumer needs, and market potential. By breaking the process down into discrete steps for understanding your external environment, internal environment, and translational analysis to strategic priority setting, you can unlock growth.

Understanding the External Environment

To effectively understand an organization's strategic priorities, you first need to develop an understanding of the external environment that the organization operates in. This involves evaluating and analyzing relevant macro trends, your industry landscape, your competitive landscape, and your customer behaviors and needs.

In terms of macro trends, you will want to stay up-to-date on key geo-political, social, and economic trends at the global level that may impact your business. For example, factors like trade policy changes, economic expansion or crisis in key markets, or major social movements related to your product offering. These type of macro trends shape consumer buying behaviors and market conditions.

Likewise, you will need to understand your specific industry landscape and dynamics deeply. This means analyzing the overall market size and historic and projected growth rates, so you can pinpoint areas of opportunity and growth potential. It also involves understanding current and emerging innovations, technologies, and offerings to remain competitive. You should also stay informed around current and planned recruiting, hiring, and work practices related to talent in your industry.

Additionally, monitoring your competitive landscape is crucial for identifying threats or opportunities relative to current and potential alternative product or business offerings. Learn about competitors and emerging disruptive players through competitive intelligence gathering. Focus on determining competitors' strengths, weaknesses, product portfolio, pricing strategies, market share, growth rates, and customer base to get a complete picture of the competitive landscape.

Lastly, gathering qualitative and quantitative consumer insights through research should form a core part of understanding your external environment. Learn about customer demographics, behaviors, attitudes, needs, values, fears, purchasing criteria and decision making processes through surveys, interviews, focus groups and data analysis.

Understanding the Internal Environment

In addition to the external environment, strategic priorities must also be grounded in a strong comprehension of the internal organizational environment. Specific areas to analyze here include financial performance trends, operational capabilities, and your organization's unique institutional knowledge.

Examine historical and current internal sales and financial performance data to spot trends, growth trajectories, seasonal variability, cash flow health, profitability per product line or customer segment, and other indicators of efficiency. Comparing internal data to wider industry benchmarks can further enhance your analysis. This enables data-driven strategic planning and goal setting.

Additionally, objectively assess existing operational capabilities related to production systems, technologies utilized, distribution channels and networks, supply chains, real estate assets, and talent. Identify strengths to leverage and gaps or inefficiencies that may need to be addressed. Also determine current and near future capacity levels to handle increased demand. This ensures you can deliver on strategic plans.

Also tap into secondary research and existing institutional knowledge across public policy shifts, government data, trade association findings, historical consumer research, and past strategy documents or meeting notes. This information can reveal what has previously worked well or failed for your organization and where institutional knowledge gaps exist.

Collecting and Validating Consumer Insights

To determine what information is needed to sufficiently support an organization's strategic planning process, the first critical step is conducting a consumer insights audit. This allows you to objectively assess the state of existing consumer knowledge across previous plans and research initiatives.

Specifically, closely evaluate the most recent 1-2 strategic plans to gauge how effectively consumer insights were incorporated and influenced decision making. Pinpoint which research data points or conclusions had the biggest impact on shaping strategy. Also identify any consumer information that proved irrelevant or ineffective for strategic decisions. This reveals current consumer knowledge strengths and weaknesses.

Additionally, the audit should categorize all existing insights into 3 buckets: 1) reliable and relevant insights that can inform the upcoming planning process as-is, 2) insights that are still viable but require some updating, and 3) clear gaps in consumer understanding that need to be addressed by initiating new research projects.

Cataloging information in this manner spotlights available knowledge to leverage and allows you to prioritize bridging gaps through additional consumer research in high impact areas for strategic planning.

While auditing, also examine the relative age and shelf life of existing insights. Consumer behaviors, attitudes, needs and market forces can shift abruptly. So insights over 2 years old risk lacking relevance for strategic decisions aiming to align operations with current realities.

Schedule follow up validation for aging but still viable insights at least 6 months prior to commencing strategic planning. Quickly confirm continued accuracy through targeted consumer surveys, interviews, or focus groups.

Likewise, address key information gaps revealed in the audit over this same 6 month time period. Initiate quantitative and qualitative primary research through avenues like online surveys, in-person focus groups, expert panels, and third party data purchases to build necessary knowledge in time to inform priorities and decision making.

Following this process ensures the planning process is grounded in a combination of freshly validated insights and urgent knowledge gains around consumer behaviors and market dynamics. Reliable, applicable consumer inputs drive strategy resonance with current conditions for superior execution and outcomes.

Setting Strategic Priorities

With a firm handle on the external landscape and internal environment, you can then bring everything together to identify target areas aligning with organizational strengths and market opportunities. These then form the strategic priorities to orient operations around.

For example, data may show strong growth in a customer segment where you hold competitive advantages and have production capacity to expand. This would represent a strategic priority for investment and focus. On the contrary, declining industry revenue on a particular product line paired with internal inefficiencies would suggest deprioritizing that area.

The goal is to ground strategic priorities in real data and insights versus assumptions or guesswork. This requires synthesizing both external consumer, industry and macro level insights and internal performance data and capabilities. Additionally, identifying priorities means determining what not to prioritize just as much as what to go after. Making data-driven strategic trade-offs allows for resources to concentrate where opportunity meets organizational abilities.

Following this process, you can derive a targeted yet flexible set of strategic priorities centered on seizing growth potential from market opportunities where you possess existing or attainable competitive advantages. The external landscape should inform what the priorities are, while internal capabilities and constraints inform how you will deliver on them. Revisiting and adjusting these priorities regularly as new data emerges ensures you remain aligned to realize your growth potential as the competitive environment inevitably evolves.

Building Trust and Delivering Value

As a sales professional, establishing trust with your customers is paramount. By clearly communicating how you earn and maintain their trust, focusing on the value you provide, and practicing responsible data stewardship, you can build strong customer connections and ultimately boost outcomes.

Let's start with value. Your customers need to understand the tangible benefits they gain from engaging with you. What problems do you solve? What needs do you meet? How will working with you improve their lives or businesses? Make these outcomes crystal clear from the outset. People are more willing to share personal information and insights when they recognize their involvement directly enhances the experience and results they receive.

Next, address trust through your principles and practices regarding customer data. Be upfront about precisely how data will and won't be used. reassure customers that their privacy and security are top priorities. For example, will you use data solely to enhance the customer experience, or might it also be leveraged for commercial advantage? Promise to take responsibility if any issues arise and commit to strict enforcement of privacy standards across your organization. People deserve transparency about these important issues.

Lead by example in your industry. Adobe exemplifies this approach with their guiding principle succinctly: "We are committed to data privacy and sensitive to how we use data. Responsible use of customer data can create greater experiences, but the second we start using it to gain tactical advantage, we've missed the mark." Adobe's focus on putting customers first through values-driven data practices clearly resonates.

Make trust and value your priorities as well. Communicate openly about why customers should feel confident engaging with you and how doing so directly improves outcomes that matter most to them. With clarity on approach and benefit, prioritizing privacy, and responsible data stewardship, you lay the groundwork for beneficial long-term partnerships built on mutual understanding and trust. Remember - your customers are people, not products. Treat their information, insights, and experiences with the care and respect they deserve. Upholding the highest ethical standards helps ensure continued opportunities to deliver value together.

Continue to Seemlessly Gather Customer Insights

Rather than treating customer insight gathering as a separate process, integrate it into your existing customer engagement touchpoints. This allows you to extract privileged learnings while simultaneously creating value for customers across interactions like service inquiries, purchases, product usage, and more. The key is ensuring customers feel their needs are being met rather than only data being extracted.

For example, fast fashion retailer Zara trains retail employees to provide excellent style guidance to customers while tracking purchasing choices, product inquiries, sizing questions, and other cues. By compiling these frontline observations with granular sales data analytics, Zara keeps pulse on exactly what shoppers prefer to inform new designs. This ultimately improves customer experiences through well-aligned inventory and fashion cycles.

The real advantage comes from actually applying the harvested insights to adapt your value proposition. Build capabilities for quickly aggregating insights, spotting patterns or changes, and implementing operational adjustments, product enhancements, or even entirely new offerings. Allowing Zara to analyze insight patterns regularly to swiftly modify logistics pipelines, production volumes, marketing campaigns, and designer working plans. So rather than just documenting customer preferences, they actualize them into delivered products within weeks. This precision matching of supply and demand unlocks major efficiency and customer satisfaction gains.

Ultimately, the goal is creating a feedback loop where insights influence enhancements that improve future customer engagements. This in turns nets even stronger insights to drive the next round of value creating adaptations. It becomes a self-reinforcing cycle anchored in listening to and activating on privileged customer learnings in an ongoing manner.

Leveraging Customer Insights Across the Organization

Building systems to capture and apply customer insights can significantly boost outcomes when done right. Rather than treating these privileged learnings as a one-off input, truly maximize their value by strategically "wiring" them throughout key operations.

Of course, innovation always comes to mind as an area ripe for insights integration. But don't stop there. Consider how customer data might affect your investments, team structures, processes and more. Use insights to holistically re-evaluate business fundamentals over time, not just introduce small changes.

Salesforce exemplifies this approach. From the start, they prioritized building trust to gain a deeper understanding of user needs. This allows constant product improvement directly informed by on-platform behavior. It also fuels new industry clouds tailored for specific segments.

This dynamic exchange of value and insights establishes a self-sustaining flywheel. Customers readily share perspectives knowing it enhances their own experiences. In turn, these learnings nourish Salesforce's ongoing evolution and expansion. It's no coincidence they achieved unprecedented growth—leveraging customer data at their core in a virtuous cycle of trust, insights and innovation.

As the foundation of your privileged insights system, focus on developing genuine partnerships rooted in transparency, responsibility and success for all involved. Look beyond singular metrics to holistic return on relationship measures. Consider impacts well beyond a product feature too—where else might customer views spur change across your sales, service, finance and more?

View insights not as a siloed asset but veins connecting your organization's heart. Infuse stratetgies, decisions and development with real-world perspectives so your offerings continue addressing precisely what clients need. Adapt structures flexibly as understanding grows deeper over time.

When customer interests consistently inform and guide your work, true-flywheels take flight, propelling both parties forward together through ever-strengthening bonds built on demonstrated value for all.

Leveraging Insights to Guide Strategic Decision Making

Developing a clear strategic vision requires understanding customers, markets and industry trends better than anyone. By systematically researching these dynamics and aligning findings with your planning process, you can make fully informed decisions to advance your priorities.

Define your customer profile by exploring who they are, what matters most to them and how behaviors are evolving. What shifts may lie ahead based on broader forces? Thoroughly comprehending these realities helps ensure you meet changing needs.

Ground all initiatives in your unique value proposition - the core benefit you deliver. Constantly examine its relevance and effective communication from the customer point of view. Strengthening this focus reinforces your brand against competitors.

Forecast demand by gaining clarity on what customers will buy, why and how to boost engagement. Remove practical barriers by identifying limitations. With data-backed projections, strategize growth proactively rather than reacting to surprises.

Evaluate your category landscape to determine optimal brand positioning. Benchmark offerings against rivals based on customer criteria. Map preferred awareness, consideration and purchase pathways. Factor real shopping behaviors into media strategies and the customer journey.

Refine pricing models with a rigorous examination of budget allocation and sensitivity levels. Test promotional impact versus competitors. Investigate value perceptions around bundling, subscriptions or other tailored options to meet true affordability and satisfaction standards.

Make insights central to high-level discussions by seamlessly integrating findings into your planning cycle. Let customer realities inform critical questions, spark new angles and validate direction. With research as your North Star, ensure decisions steadily advance the interests of those you serve while strengthening your role in the market.

Chapter Nine

Personalizing the Sales Experience

C reating a personalized sales experience tailored to each prospective customer is pivotal for making meaningful connections, building trust, demonstrating understanding of unique needs and priorities, and ultimately closing more deals. This involves gathering insight into prospects ahead of sales conversations and using that intel to customize messaging and solutions for every individual.

The first critical step is researching prospects before interactions to uncover background, challenges, and preferences. Sources like LinkedIn, company websites, and news articles provide helpful context. Additionally, connect with stakeholders inside the prospect's organization through warm introductions whenever possible. This enables you to start conversations already understanding key details about motivations and pain points.

Equipped with targeted research on prospects' industries, roles, goals and obstacles, you can develop truly personalized messaging for each. This means tweaking how you frame the value you provide to resonate based on each prospect's reality. Get specific by calling out which features solve their very particular needs or speaking directly to growth opportunities in their unique market landscape.

Further personalize sales experiences by using prospect insights to deliver highly tailored solution recommendations. Provide options that speak their language, incorporate familiar tools or vendors when possible and address their exact business requirements. This degree of specialization demonstrates you grasp and respect their individual contexts and builds credibility. It shows you aim to enable their success versus making a one-size-fits all sale.

The proof behind personalization is hard metrics showing it works. Activity track prospect engagement, win rates and deal sizes for customized sales interactions versus generic ones. Tools like CRMs quantify the impact personalization has in boosting positive sales outcomes. Leverage the data to guide refinements to your process.

Personalizing every touchpoint in the sales cycle from initial research through final follow-ups is no longer optional - it's essential for competitive differentiation and sales success. It undoubtedly requires more work but delivers exponential gains in prospect trust, solution relevancy and ultimately revenue. Now is the time to start customizing conversations and blowing past status quo results.

Provide Your Contacts with Relevant Information

Contacts crave communications tailored to their unique needs and priorities. Generic outreach simply won't captivate attention. To cut through the noise and drive engagement, provide contacts with ultra-relevant information personalized to their contexts. This requires understanding individuals' preferences and challenges before sending recommendations their way.

Getting to Know Your Contacts

The foundation for relevance is insight into what matters most to each contact. Develop profiles documenting individual responsibilities, goals and pain points. Also track content they access, session length, shares and other digital body language. Look for themes pointing to priorities and preferences. Regularly update notes as contacts' roles and interests evolve.

Crafting Customized Content

Equipped with robust contact profiles, you can create content personalized to be timely and useful for each individual. For example, send focused ebooks, articles, whitepapers, event invites, and product recommendations mapped to challenges they're currently facing in their unique roles. Repurpose evergreen content by putting their particular spin on it. Personalized subject lines with their names capture attention better as well.

Automating Relevance at Scale

Delivering tailored communications manually has limitations. Marketing automation platforms scale relevance using algorithms to match content topics, formats and cadences to contact preferences automatically. Feed in rich contact data and rules to orchestrate hyper-relevant nurture streams. Continuously refine based on engagement analytics.

Getting Personalization Right

Avoid mistaking invasive targeting for true personalization. Keep customized content focused squarely on enabling contacts' goals rather than promoting products randomly. Misaligned messaging damages trust and engagement. Create relevance rooted in understanding people's needs first.

The fiercest competition for contacts' limited attention is ultra-relevant information. To rise above the noise, demonstrate you grasp unique contexts and priorities in your outreach. Personalized content, offers and recommendations tailored to individual needs cultivate lasting connections and opportunities.

Crafting Custom Sales Presentations

PowerPoint decks no longer captivate prospects' attention. To demonstrate deep understanding of buyers' unique contexts and priorities throughout sales conversations, leading professionals employ interactive presentations personalized to individual needs. Research shows sales content tailored to specific customers' situations can prove up to 25% more effective at communicating value. The ability to visualize solutions aligned to organizations' objectives also fuels deeper connections and higher win rates. Embracing custom presentations is now imperative for sales success.

Curating Contextual Insight on Buyers

The foundation for impactful personalized presentations is contextual insight into prospects ahead of meetings. Thoroughly research target roles, industries and regional landscapes prospective customers operate within. Review priorities, growth goals, pain points and key performance indicators that matter most to their business. This immersion shapes initial customizations like relevant case studies and market trends. Also connect with stakeholders inside prospects' companies through warm introductions whenever possible. Frank conversations enable sales teams to surface hot buttons and frame narratives most likely to resonate.

Co-Creating Value in Real-Time

Equipped with research on buyers' situations, sales reps can co-create truly tailored presentations in live meetings. Initially walk through slide frameworks focused on challenges prospects face daily in their roles and tailor talking points to their circumstances. Then utilize interactive tools allowing prospects to build custom views of solutions on the fly based on variables unique to their organization like headcount, average contract values and growth targets. These specialized views displayed in real-time quantify the value you provide more credibly and empathetically.

Getting Granular with Personalization

Drill down to granular personalization by using customized AV materials, conversational language familiar to the prospect's industry, regionalized data, and other subtle but meaningful tweaks. Send branded presentations ahead of meetings for prospects to self-navigate too. The more bespoke each interaction, the greater differentiation achieved. Custom styling matching prospects' corporate identities also reinforces positioning your organization as an extension of their team.

Automating Personalization at Scale

While manual customization sets a gold standard, leverage technology like sales engagement platforms to personalize components of presentations at scale when needed. Feed profiles on prospects' contexts into systems and build modular decks with variant slides tailored to vertical, role type, region etc. Then use rules-based logic to automatically assemble slides suited to individuals. Continuously hone based on real-time buying signals.

Calculating the ROI of Custom Content

Demonstrating solid ROI cements the case for personalization. For each prospect, track deal progression and win rates when using tailored presentations versus generic ones. Document how customized experiences shrink sales cycles by building immediate relevance. Look at residual sales from elevated intimacy and trust as well. Hard metrics proving custom content accelerates opportunities and revenue compared to one-size-fits all materials make ironclad arguments.

Personalized sales presentations demonstrating deep understanding of what makes buyers unique secure more appointments, build authentic connections and consistently close more deals. The additional work of creating targeted visuals pays off exponentially by enabling customer-specific perspectives on value. As virtual selling becomes ubiquitous, taking the time to customize interactions moves from nice-to-have to baseline standard.

Personalizing the Customer Experience in Sales Meetings

Customers today expect companies to understand them individually. Rather than generic pitches, people want interactions tailored specifically for their unique situation. A 2018 Adobe survey found over two-thirds of consumers feel it's important for content to adjust automatically based on what's relevant for them personally in real-time. This level of personalization has become a basic requirement.

During sales meetings, focus on envisioning improved experiences in the prospect's daily life, not just product benefits. Really listen to learn exactly what matters most to each individual. For example, health insurance advisors need to create dynamic, personalized dialog. As conversations evolve, presentations should visually provide customized details for the prospect's specific needs and background. If an advisor understands a prospect wants coverage for certain health issues or activities, they can demonstrate policies meeting those needs. As more information is shared, the recommendations should adapt seamlessly.

Customers appreciate efforts to recommend solutions fitting their personal preferences revealed over discussion. Sales meetings thrive on one-on-one understanding and attention, not prefabricated monologues. As technology assists advisors in tailoring communications and content live, companies succeed based on personalized customer care. Focusing sales discussions around individual prospects' objectives and realities builds strong relationships and satisfaction over generic approaches.

Personalizing Your Sales Approach

Personalization is no longer just a nice-to-have — it's a must-have. Research shows 96% of customers are more likely to engage with personalized messaging. Clearly, taking the time to tailor communications to individual prospects is rapidly becoming essential.

By framing sales conversations around demonstrated customer challenges and goals, reps build necessary trust and relevance early. We will share approaches for then sustaining personalized momentum from initial outreach through demos and follow-ups. Tactics cover manifesting core storytelling principles as applied to the prospect's specific journey.

The Key to Sales Success: Preparation

Preparation is the key to success. This rings true for sales professionals aiming to personalize their outreach. Before contacting a prospect, dedicate time to researching them and their organization. Build a picture by asking questions like:

- What are their interests and how do they spend their time?

- What challenges might they face and how can you help address them?

- What is the structure and culture of their organization?

- Can you learn anything about their personality and preferred communication style?

This information allows you to tailor your introductory outreach. A startup employee likely has very different priorities than an executive at a long-established company. Your prospects are not one-size-fits-all, so your initial approach should not be either.

Use professional sites like LinkedIn to research prospects. Spend two to three minutes reviewing available information to inform your personalized intro. Visiting someone's profile means they may also view yours, facilitating familiarity.

With insight into a prospect's role, interests and company, you can demonstrate professional interest by referencing relevant details. This levels the playing field for a cold outreach by highlighting shared connections. It also enables you to speak directly to likely challenges and priorities using language that resonates.

Conclude your customized intro by posing an open-ended question or highlighting opportunity for future dialogue. As sales development rep Stephanie Diaz recommends, "I go over pain points and solutions, conclude with a question, or tell them I look forward to chatting about their individual challenges or pain points." This warm, consultative approach makes prospects receptive to learning more.

The key is letting your research guide how you frame the initial contact to signal personalization. This small investment of time pays dividends by driving more qualified conversations. Preparation is indeed fundamental to succeed in today's increasingly personalized sales landscape.

Direct the Conversation With Purpose

A little direction goes a long way in sales calls. Before dialing, clearly define the purpose of the conversation and prepare to articulate it to prospects. Example call objectives include:

- Learning about specific individual challenges

- Discovering current solutions used

- Scheduling demonstrations

- Presenting special offers

Outlining the "why" helps customize dialogues to address customer priorities while aligning with your goals. It also informs logical next actions post-call to advance opportunities.

Progress Prospects with Purpose

Well-defined call purposes prevent wasting time on repetitive conversations or unnecessary asides. Instead, they enable forwarding the prospect along the sales funnel efficiently. Start broad by gathering intel through consultative questioning. Then, redefine the purpose as needed to transition discussions toward demos or pricing. Refining the "why" as conversations progress lets you pivot while maintaining personalized relevance.

Enhance Understanding with Tech

Supplement call purpose clarity by streaming conversations through AI-powered software. Intelligent transcription with pattern recognition can help quickly highlight key prospect challenges, priorities, and pain points. These insights further inform personalized next steps after hanging up and tighten feedback loops to refine the "why" for future calls. Technology supports manual efforts to stay focused on the purposes driving individual conversations.

Articulating a clear "why" before engaging prospects personalizes discussions by aligning with their needs. It also lends direction to propel opportunities forward post-call. Defining and redefining purpose is essential to customize conversations while progressing them towards desired outcomes.

Craft a Compelling Demo Narrative

Your demo is a chance to show the impact your solution can make, not just highlight features. Think of it as telling a story, with the prospect as the lead character facing challenges your offering helps resolve.

Start by learning your prospect's priorities and professional responsibilities. What goals are driving their search for a better way? Make sure to understand their unique situation and perspective.

Spotlight the Lead Character

Begin the demo introducing this key character. Share just enough about their role and objectives to set the scene. Think of your prospect as the protagonist. Open by highlighting their goals, objectives and responsibilities. This hooks attention while immediately personalizing the narrative.

Set the Scene

To fully immerse your prospect in the unfolding narrative, provide rich details about their work environment and industry setting. Bringing these contextual elements to light helps position them at the center of a story they'll find meaningful.

Paint a picture of their company - discuss its size, structure, culture and values. Help the prospect envision how these organizational characteristics shape their daily priorities and challenges.

Give visibility to typical workflows and processes too. Illustrate the frontlines of operations and how your lead character currently functions within them. Bringing routines and methods to the fore sets the operational stage.

Additionally, introduce pertinent industry dynamics. Highlight competitive forces, technology trends or other transformations impacting their sector. Situating market conditions and disruptions the prospect contends with helps justify their quest for superior solutions.

With organizational and environmental backdrops now established, you've fully situated your lead character. Their circumstances come into focus, bringing purpose to what follows in your demonstration. Each subsequent feature connects directly to nuances already spotlighted, forming a cohesive narrative tied intrinsically to the prospect's reality. By thoroughly setting the scene, you empower them to imagine overcoming obstacles as the hero of your story unfolding.

Introduce Conflict

Every great tale requires adversity to overcome. Now it's time to introduce tension within your prospect's experience by spotlighting real pain points revealed in earlier discovery talks.

Specifically call out frustrations hampering their efficiency, productivity and ability to hit goals. Draw from earlier conversations to emphasize tangible challenges around processes, resources, change management or other hurdles currently obstructing success.

Bring problems like unnecessary work, lack of visibility, wasted time or delays to the forefront. Presenting these as obstacles your lead character grapples with daily engages their understanding while priming them for solutions.

You may also introduce outer conflict stemming from industry pressures. Highlight how unresolved issues inhibit adapting to evolving customer needs, emerging competitors or broader sector shifts threatening viability.

Positioning such recognized struggles at the center establishes a compelling problem for your hero to solve. It primes the prospect to welcome your assistance by demonstrating hard issues currently defying independent resolution through existing means.

With impediments and tension firmly established, you've created motivation for what's to come. Your prospect now relates personally to the struggles accentuated, eager to witness prospects for relief through your offering's involvement in the next phase of the story.

Offer the Resolution

You've set the stage and introduced conflict tailored closely to your prospect's reality. Now it's time for the triumphant finale - proving how your solution liberates their potential.

Walk through capabilities in a way that directly addresses each pain previously called out. Demonstrate step-by-step how your offering removes obstacles, streamlines routines and supplies new superpowers. Show tangible impacts like saved time, improved oversight and collaborative strength.

Emphasize values like ease-of-use, flexibility and intuitive design aligned with organization preferences. Highlight outcomes helping workers reach new heights of productivity while seamlessly adapting to change.

Culminate the narrative by connecting achievements back to your protagonist's key goals. Display enthusiastic users with testimonials paralleling details from your prospect's environment and challenges. Bring the story full circle, resolving all conflicts to inspire a vision of success.

Through this custom-crafted journey, your prospect now witnesses light ahead thanks to your solution's involvement in their tale. By resolving struggles so thoughtfully tied to their situation, you paint a compelling future actively seeking their participation in writing the next chapter.

Personalize the Follow-Up

As you wrap up the demo, emphasize next actions tailored to the prospect's specific interests.

My advice is to shine the spotlight on no more than 3 beneficial features. Rather than reciting all benefits, focus follow up discussions uncovering untapped potential the prospect found most compelling based on their unique role challenges. Personalizing discussions in this manner perpetuates their envisioning success through continued involvement.

Promote next steps experientially, whether pilot testing a favorite module, arranging customized demos touching on favored solutions, or scheduling further discovery meetings to explore evolving needs. Leverage takeaways continually sharpening your comprehension of this lead character and company circumstances.

View this first demonstration as the opening of an ongoing narrative. Maintain focus on resolutely addressing conflicts core to the prospect's journey through attentive engagement. Keep actively evolving your understanding of what drives them as roles and responsibilities potentially change over time.

By keeping dialogue personalized through active listening, regular check-ins and tailored follow ups, you sustain momentum transforming this sales opportunity into a long term partnership story still unfolding through collaborative adventures ahead. Demos should tell stories starring prospects while spotlighting contexts and challenges. This narrative approach makes personalization intuitive, memorable and compelling. Put yourself in the customer's shoes to deliver the perfect pitch.

Chapter Ten

Innovating Your Sales Process

O ver the years, many sales methodologies have been introduced in an attempt to systemize and optimize the selling process, including Consultative Selling, SPIN Selling, Strategic Selling, and more recently, Challenger Selling. While these approaches have merits, they also have limitations in today's customer-centric business landscape. Companies need sales processes that are flexible, adaptive and truly focused on the customer.

Traditional sales methods tend to promote standardized, one-size-fits-all processes for interacting with customers. However, buyers today are more informed and empowered in the purchasing process. They expect salespeople to understand their specific business goals and challenges. This requires innovating the sales model to be more consultative, collaborative and customer-centric.

Additionally, many established sales training programs emphasize product knowledge and scripted pitch techniques over developing authentic customer relationships. But scripted pitches feel inauthentic to buyers and fail to provide real value. An innovative, customer-first sales approach is needed.

Core Elements of Innovative Selling

Innovative selling involves more than novel products - it's an innovative mindset applied throughout the entire customer experience. At its heart are several core principles:

Understand customer needs thoroughly. Adopt a consultative, curiosity-driven approach to discovering needs beyond what's explicitly stated. Listen actively and explore underlying motivations to grasp needs as deeply as possible.

Craft creative solutions. Don't limit thinking to current offerings. Brainstorm new ideas that could resolve needs in entirely novel yet practical ways. Collaborate with customers on co-creating customized approaches.

Remain adaptable to change. Monitor evolving business environments and pain points. Modify strategies proactively based on dynamic realities to sustain relevance over time. Welcome challenges as opportunities for improvement.

This consultative,Outside-In approach makes sales professionals valued advisors through life-long relationships built on solving problems flexibly and progressing jointly on innovative journeys.

Understand Your Customer's Business Strategy and Value Proposition to Their Customers

Success in sales today requires moving beyond product pitches and truly understanding your customer's business strategy and value proposition. Only with deep insight into how your customer creates and delivers value can you become a strategic partner rather than merely a supplier. Thisarticle outlines how to research your customer's business, have strategic dialogue with executives, and leverage your learning to provide genuine value.

Conducting Research for Strategic Insight

The first step is conducting thorough research on your customer's company, competitors, industry dynamics and value proposition. Look for press releases, earning call transcripts, industry reports and news mentioning your customer. Strive to understand details like:

- Their target customers and demographic trends

- Core differentiators and value propositions

- Competitive threats they face

- Key technologies or innovations driving their market

- Cost pressures, supply chain issues or other risks

This high-level research gives crucial context for zeroing in on their strategy and customer value proposition.

Engaging in Strategic Dialogue

Next, arrange conversations with key contacts such as executives, operations leads and technical experts. Move past small talk by asking open questions like:

- "What major objectives is your leadership focused on this year?"

- "How do you differentiate your offerings from competitors?"

- "What customer needs guide your product roadmap?"

- "What challenges might disrupt delivering value?"

As they share strategic insights, listen intently for goals, philosophies, metrics and terminology that reveal their priorities. Capture details through notes and frameworks.

Understanding Their Value Proposition

Finally, synthesize your research and dialogue learnings into an overview of their customer value proposition—how they create value for customers at each stage. Map detailed customer journeys to reveal pain points and value gaps your offering could address. This deep understanding becomes invaluable for presenting aligned solutions instead of disjointed products.

By dedicating time upfront to understand your customer's strategy, priorities and customer value proposition, you transform from a commodity seller to a strategic partner. These insights make collaborating on tailored solutions possible throughout our sales and customer lifecycle.

Generating and Assessing Innovative Sales Process Improvements

With a solid understanding of your current sales process strengths and pain points, you can start actively ideating and evaluating process innovations to better meet customer needs. This article outlines techniques for generating ideas, as well as key criteria to assess proposed innovations to determine strategic fit and practical feasibility before testing and implementation.

Idea Generation Techniques

Several creativity boosting approaches help uncover fresh perspectives and possibilities for enhancing your sales workflow. Useful ideation methods include:

- Brainstorming sessions to tap your team's insights

- Mind mapping to visualize innovative concepts

- Looking outside your industry for sales models worth emulating

- Prototyping mock solution workflows to showcase future-state ideas

- Surveying top customers about process frustrations

The key is generating a high volume and diversity of possibilities without initially judging quality. Seeking ideas from those directly interfacing with customers daily yields the most relevance.

Assessing Ideas Strategically

With a list of potential process innovations, systematically determine which rise to the top for testing and implementation. Assess each against criteria including:

- Feasibility - Technical difficulty, staff capabilities required

- Cost - Expected development/ rollout budget needed

- Potential impact - Could it drive revenue, retention or efficiency gains?

- Customer insight alignment - Does it address identified pain points?

- Strategic fit - Would it further overall sales goals and priorities?

Catalog all evaluations to reference. Involve sales operations leaders in aligning selections with objectives for the overall sales workflow optimization roadmap.

Ongoing Innovation Cadence

Continually inject new thinking into enhancing your sales processes to meet evolving customer expectations. Build regular ideation and evaluation cycles into your improvement frameworks to keep momentum.

For instance, add ideation sessions focusing on different stages of the sales funnel as standing agenda items for team meetings. Or host an annual "process innovation jam" where creative customers also provide input. Maintaining an innovation cadence ensures your critical sales processes stay ahead.

Challenging Customers to Innovate and Evolve

While most customers prefer maintaining the status quo, salespeople play a crucial role in constructively challenging current mindsets and processes. Asking thoughtful, provocative questions encourages organizations to re-evaluate strategies in light of evolving market dynamics. This prevents stagnation that could render them obsolete overtime. Here's how to tactfully push customers beyond existing perspectives without alienating them.

Understanding the Tendency Toward Inertia

First, recognize most customers are wired toward inertia and reluctance to change. Making major modifications requires substantial effort and risk. It's easier to continue established patterns, especially when performance seems satisfactory currently.

However, the pace of change across industries today demands that even well-run companies regularly revisit strategies to ensure alignment with emerging trends, technologies and buyer expectations. Salespeople who stimulus productive discomfort through insightful questioning provide a valuable external perspective.

Asking Constructive, Thought-Provoking Questions

When meeting with key customer contacts, prepare open-ended questions to challenge status quo thinking, such as:

- "How might shifting demographics change your value proposition overtime?"

- "What innovative offerings from adjacent spaces could disrupt your firm?"

- "How could a new platform model open untapped market potential?"

- "Where might enhancements around personalization and self-service be warranted?"

These queries highlight unknowns and areas for potential improvement. Be highly attentive to responses looking for signals more exploration around innovations may be warranted.

Respectfully Encouraging Re-Evaluation

Handle resulting dialogue with care and empathy. Change initiatives require investment and risk. Avoid seeming overly pushy or critical. Instead, position exploring adjustments in light of external change as an opportunity to get ahead of curves through controlled, incremental pilots.

Share examples of admired firms evolving strategically over time. Acknowledge you don't have all the answers but are eager to collaborate on brainstorming possibilities through an innovation lens. The goal is opening minds, not forcing predefined solutions.

Understanding Key Trends to Translate Strategic Insights

Paying attention to emerging trends allows salespeople to provide genuine strategic value to customer organizations. By researching and translating influential developments in technology, demographics, consumer behaviors and more into relevant insights, you become a forward-thinking advisor rather than purely a product supplier. This article outlines an approach to continuously analyzing trends and crafting implications meaningful for sparking innovation with customers.

Identifying Relevant Trends

Globalization and digitization surfaces new trends continuously across markets. As a trusted partner for customers, you must actively monitor news and research around developments including:

- New platform business models or disruptive startups

- Shifts in workplace norms, especially post-pandemic

- Breakthrough technologies on the horizon for your industry

- Evolving consumer preferences and purchasing behaviors

- Changes in talent expectations and skill requirements

- Supply chain innovations that promise efficiency gains

Capture trends resonating as potentially impactful for customers in an insights database, including metadata like dates, sources and possible use cases to reference.

Translating Into Customer Impact

While an intriguing trend alone holds little value, interpreting implications for your customer's business sparks productive strategic dialogue. Prepare talking points that explain trends clearly and highlight how they might:

- Open new market opportunities or demand shifts

- Enable emerging customer experiences and business models

- Alter cost structures, productivity or competitiveness

- Require new capabilities or partnerships

- Change talent recruiting and retention approaches

Avoid generic statements. Tailor translations of trends into specific strategies, investments or innovations customers should consider in response. Cite examples of other firms evolving based on the same external signals to lend credibility.

Ongoing Advisory Dialogues

Proactively reach out to customer executives and innovation leaders to discuss trends most relevant for their business. Position yourself as an expert guide eager to translate developments into actionable responses. Over time these advisory strategy conversations cement your role as a vital ally in driving their competitiveness and evolution rather than just another commodity seller.

Fostering Autonomy to Drive Innovation

Business leaders often wonder how to spark more innovative thinking across their organizations. While many initiatives like idea competitions and hackathons have merit, research reveals that simply giving employees greater autonomy and flexibility fuels creative outcomes. When you demonstrate trust, people feel empowered to challenge status quo processes and try new approaches. This article provides guidance on allowing teams autonomy to unlock ingenuity.

The Power of Psychological Safety

What most significantly impacts whether employees go beyond their job description to question solutions and pioneer better ways? The single strongest predictor is psychological safety – feeling their ideas and risk-taking won't be harshly judged. Without autonomy and the ability to fail fast, people default to safe routines.

As a leader then, you set the tone for psychological safety on your team. Empower people with agency in how they tackle objectives. Accept smart experiments that may not pan out. Show that you welcome disruptive concepts and eager collaboration is more valued than hierarchy.

Reevaluating Processes

Additionally, systematically reassess legacy processes that limit flexibility and cause frustrations. Can aspects be streamlined or simplified to enable self-guided enhancements? Build in periodic reviews for upgrading workflows.

Invite team feedback on where more latitude would spark innovations. Grant permission to test new sequences, set aside resources for controlled pilots. Removing constraints and approval bottlenecks liberates experimentation.

Metrics Beyond Profits

When evaluating ideas and efforts, emphasize metrics like creativity, speed and user experience rather than merely short-term financial returns. Recognize that breakthroughs often involve iteration and natural missteps. Take the long view that autonomy surrounds your organization with fresh perspectives.

Make it safe to take chances and reboot approaches without pressure. As Google likes to say, allowing "space" for tinkering has unlocked some of their most game-changing products in the famous 20% time policy.

While extensive processes have their place in scaling execution, also cultivate open spaces for people to exercise creativity muscles and pioneer solutions. Enable autonomy with psychological safety, streamline outdated constraints, and celebrate invention efforts. Unleashing potential and initiative at all levels will wonderfully surprise you over time.

Implementing a Customer-Centric Process

Becoming a truly customer-centric, innovative organization requires alignment and support across all levels. Here are some key steps sales leaders can take:

Provide ongoing training: Transforming rep mindsets takes continuous learning. Train representatives to listen without bias, think beyond standard categories, and understand each customer's unique challenges, priorities and desired outcomes.

Equip reps for discovery: Give salespeople robust tools to thoroughly research accounts and comprehensively document customer insights. Enable insightful discovery discussions through collaborative digital workspaces customized for each buyer's preferences and needs.

Capture and share knowledge: Create centralized platforms allowing reps to contribute discoveries, ideas and lessons learned for industry or account-specific research. Enable learning across the organization so insights from any interation can benefit future customers.

Develop feedback channels: Solicit regular input from customers via surveys, interviews or advisory boards. Encourage open communication to identify opportunities, assess satisfaction and refine strategies based on real-world outcomes and experiences.

Measure success qualitatively: Go beyond quantitave metrics to holistically evaluate customer advocacy, relationship strength and stakeholder outcomes. View the sales process as an ongoing investment in customer-centric problem solving, not individual contract attainment.

With leadership commitment behind these capability and process enablers, your organization will cultivate the innovative sales culture modern buyers now expect throughout all engagement touchpoints.

Chapter Eleven

Aligning Customer Success and Sales

H istorically, sales and customer success teams have operated in silos, focusing solely on their own metrics and responsibilities. Sales teams concentrate on bringing in new customers and hitting revenue targets, while customer success owns retention and expansion of existing accounts. This separated structure often creates misalignment on shared goals around exceptional customer experiences, satisfaction, and overall company growth.

While sales and customer success teams have had traditionally different objectives, there is also significant overlap in their pursuits when taking a big picture view. Ultimately every employee likely shares a core goal of sustaining and expanding the business through revenue and customer growth. But without open communication, collaboration, and strategic alignment of sales and customer success teams, this overarching growth mandate suffers.

Siloed teams lead to fractured customer experiences. For example, a sales representative may promise certain onboarding services without confirming if the customer success team can deliver on those expectations. This leads to poor post-purchase experiences that hurt customer satisfaction as well as word-of-mouth referrals. Additionally, without sales and customer success insight into one another's interactions, customers get frustrated repeating needs and pain points to different company representatives.

Lack of shared customer insights also leads sales teams to focus more on short-term revenue wins over long-term customer growth. When compensated mainly on new business acquisition, sales teams prioritize prospecting over confirming current customers have successful onboarding. This disconnect means missed opportunities for expansion revenue from happy existing customers.

While differences in sales and customer success metrics, compensation incentives, and typical DNA profiles of employees in each function can make alignment difficult, shared goals around customer lifecycle success can unite these teams. Through improved communication protocols, strategy alignment, expanded incentives beyond team-specific metrics, and cross-functional collaboration opportunities, organizations can bridge the historical divide between sales and customer success.

Addressing priorities of the entire customer journey leads to improved acquisition, onboarding, expansion, retention and advocacy. Ultimately increased lifetime value of acquired customers benefits company revenue growth as well as individual contributor success across both teams. Tight collaboration early in the sales process through to ongoing account expansion ensures customers feel taken care of from initial purchase to advocacy stages.

Bridging the Sales and Customer Success Divide

Historically, sales and customer success (CS) teams have operated in separation, incentivized by contradictory metrics and disconnected processes. Sales staff concentrate solely on new customer acquisition fueled by revenue goals and short-term payouts. Meanwhile CS focuses on retention and expansion of existing accounts, aligned to longer-term customer lifetime value. This divided approach often misaligns sales and CS activities with the overarching goal of end-to-end customer lifecycle success.

While sales and CS teams have had divergent objectives, in reality every employee likely shares the core goal of sustaining and expanding the business through delighted customers and revenue growth. But without open communication, collaboration, and strategic alignment of sales and CS teams, this mutual growth mandate suffers. Ultimately fractured experiences during the buyer's journey lead to churn, missed expansion opportunities, and poor customer satisfaction.

Fortunately, organizations can bridge this historical divide by realigning sales and CS around the unified goal of customer lifecycle achievement. This requires updating strategies, processes, and incentives to reinforce shared accountability across the entire customer experience.

Why Alignment Matters for Customer Success

Frustrated customers lead to churn. When sales promises service capabilities or onboarding resources that the CS team cannot match, purchasers feel duped. These fractured experiences directly cause lack of value realization, advocacy loss, and contract cancellations down the line. Tight alignment between sales and CS prevents setting inaccurate service expectations that CS then takes the blame for missing.

Likewise, lack of shared customer insights means CS enters engagements blind to the full context of sales promises and prospect pain points. Customers get frustrated repeating their challenges and shoeshopping their existing solution to new CS reps. Shared background on the buyer journey prevents this churn risk while enabling smoother account transitions between teams.

Beyond preventing customer frustrations, collaboration presents expansion revenue opportunities. If CS maintains connections with advocates generated during the sales process, they remain informed on broader customer initiatives. This positions CS to guide successful upsell conversations when new use cases or business challenges arise. However without proper sales alignment, context on these trusted relationships and growth possibilities get lost.

Benefits of Bridging the Sales and CS Divide

1. Improved Customer Experiences

- Mitigate buying regret and value gap by matching delivery to sales promises

- Streamline transitions between teams to prevent repetition of pain points

- Coordinate contiguous insights and capabilities between siloed teams

2. Increased Retention and Expansion

- Set accurate service expectations to prevent violated trust

- Maintain visibility into emerging needs for timely expansion guidance

- Foster enduring advocate relationships for retention and referrals

3. Accelerated Time-to-Value Realization

- Involve CS earlier to align adoption to desired outcomes

- Maintain continuity between purchase expectations and onboarding

- Guide user maturity based on full context of sales conversations

Strategies to Align Customer Success and Sales Teams

Historically, sales and customer success operate in separation - misaligned on process, data, and incentives. However, shared accountability across the entire customer journey benefits revenue and loyalty goals. This requires tight strategic alignment, collaborative processes, unified data, and expanded success metrics between previously siloed teams.

Transitioning sales and customer success into unified facilitators of customer lifetime value involves updating strategies, systems, and operations across five key areas:

1. Leadership Vision and Planning

2. Cross-Functional Process Alignment

3. Unified Customer Data Environment

4. Expanded Success Metrics and Compensation

5. Embedding Collaboration in Culture and Operations

The following strategies outline how sales and customer success leaders can erode divisions between teams to enable seamless, high-growth customer experiences.

1. Leadership Vision and Planning

Without direction from executives, alignment stalls at lower management levels. The executive team must champion a cohesive vision for customer journey success with strategic planning and resources distributed appropriately between sales and customer success teams to enable that vision.

Key Actions

- Set company objective centered on complete buyer journey facilitation

- Develop joint sales and customer success strategy roadmap

- Provision teams appropriately to match strategic priorities

- Define and reinforce shared vision in corporate communications

2. Cross-Functional Process Alignment

Inconsistent processes between sales and customer success cause poor hand-offs, knowledge gaps, and fragmented experiences. A coordinated methodology must exist around account transitions, intelligence sharing, and customer communications.

Key Actions

- Map end-to-end customer journey with experience gaps

- Identify collaboration touchpoints across the lifecycle

- Build account transition protocols and customer intelligence sharing

- Schedule periodic review cadence for continuous process optimization

3. Unified Customer Data Environment

Disjointed customer data prevents visibility into complete account history and truths. Consolidating intelligence onto a centralized platform provides universal access and a single source of truth across sales, service, and success.

Key Actions

- Audit existing data platforms and access among teams

- Define universal vs. specialized customer data needs

- Implement integrated CRM and intelligence architecture

- Provide platform training and establish data governance roles

4. Expanded Success Metrics and Compensation

Departmental incentives fuel internal competition and poor collaboration. Reward mechanisms must reinforce customer journey success, not just niche KPIs, with a balance of short and long-term metrics.

Key Actions

- Weight compensation balanced around customer lifetime value

- Expand key performance metrics beyond individual team goals

- Apply experiential health scoring to complement financials

- Incentivize cross-team collaboration for shared wins

5. Embedding Collaboration into Culture and Operations

Even with protocols and platforms for coordination, persistent silo mentalities undermine joint success. Reinforcing interconnectedness through workplace collaboration makes unity an inherent component of daily interactions and company identity.

Key Actions

- Spotlight cross-team wins in corporate messaging

- Facilitate mentoring programs and rotations across teams

- Host recurring touchpoints and joint team building exercises

- Design office space for cross-functional mingling

Account Transition Best Practices

Within the above strategies, effective methods for passing customer batons between sales and onboarding prove particularly vital to maintaining experience cohesion. Involving customer success earlier in sales conversations helps discern service capabilities, establish SLAs, and confirm executive advocacy that persists through renewal conversations.

- Define a timeline, knowledge transfer requirements, communication norms, and optimal medium between account stakeholders in the transition process.

- Routine touchpoints to exchange account insights, improvement ideas, and solution design conversations uphold a living ecosystem of collaboration.

- Explicitly mapping process and expectation accountability across sales, onboarding, and ongoing retention prevents confusion on role ownership.

While differences between sales and customer success teams intrinsically exist, cultivating shared accountability and capabilities across the entire customer journey stands critical to facilitating modern subscription business models. Developing tight strategic alignment, collaborative culture, unified data, and broad incentives ultimately benefits revenue through substantially improved customer experiences and mutually reinforced team success.

Achieving Customer Success Over Closed Deals

Shifting to a customer-centric model requires adjusting performance indicators away from short-term deals metrics toward leading indicators of lifetime customer value and loyalty. Consider metrics like:

- Retention rates: Measure continued engagement over time as a key driver of ROI.

- Customer advocacy/promoter scores: Gauge willingness to recommend and refer new partners.

- Account expansion: Track additional revenue, services adopted and share of wallet gains within existing customers.

This moves sales compensation focus toward fostering long-term success, not fleeting quarterly wins. Relationship maintenance also elevates in priority through:

- Business reviews: Proactively conduct periodic health checks, roadmap alignments and satisfaction surveys.

- Change management planning: Coach customers through evolution, helping navigate transitions smoothly.

- Partner programs: Develop collaborative onboarding, incentives and enablement for referrals/channel expansion.

Strong post-purchase support provides ongoing evidence of genuine value added through continued involvement. Customer-centric reps act as enablers invested in buyer prosperity, not detached contractors walking away after signatures. Prioritizing the human relationships yields exponentially greater returns in this model optimized for long-term success together.

Aligning Sales and Customer Success for Seamless Partnerships

Coordinating sales and customer success teams is essential for delivering unified customer experiences and driving continual growth. By optimizing cross-functional collaboration and leveraging technologies, organizations can eliminate silos between departments.

Fostering Collaboration

Collaboration is important for sharing knowledge that enhances the customer experience. Teams should be co-located to facilitate informal discussions where they can exchange customer insights, feedback, and best practices. Holding regular cross-functional meetings gives teams opportunities for education, relationship building, and problem solving together. A CRM is also key - it provides a single source of truth that allows teams to easily access account information for cooperation across stages.

Defining Clear Processes

Clear processes are important for ensuring smooth handoffs between teams. Sales should introduce new customers to their dedicated success manager to establish that relationship. Teams should also conduct post-sale reviews jointly. This allows success experts to provide early renewal predictions to sales, giving them time to address any risks. It also informs success strategies as sales keeps them updated on prospects and new opportunities.

Aligning Goals and Incentives

Aligning incentives prevents siloed behaviors by making long-term success a shared priority. Compensation should be tied to metrics like renewals, expansions, and promotions to referral programs. This encouragesteams to support each other's efforts rather than just focusing on their own departments.

Conducting Shared Reviews

Joint reviews provide opportunities for collaboration. During post-sale assessments, success insights can help sales better understand customer needs. And sales updates aid success managers in developing customized strategies. It also promotes relationship building between teams.

Leveraging Customer Understanding

By sharing knowledge regularly, teams can develop a unified understanding of mutual customers. Success interactions provide first-hand feedback that sales can use for improving future presentations. And sales prospect data helps success better engage customers pre-sale and focus renewal efforts.

Measuring Collaboratively

Using balanced metrics from both departments presents leadership with a complete view ofperformance. Customer health metrics alongside traditional sales KPIs facilitate observing ROI from collaboration while identifying areas for improvement.

By breaking silos through processes, incentives, and technological enablement focused on seamless partnerships, organizations can elevate customer experiences and outcomes consistently across all touchpoints.

Chapter Twelve

Conclusion: Sustaining Customer Centricity for Enduring Sales Success

D elivering standout customer experiences fueling advocacy and lifetime loyalty requires a sales organization fixated on continuously understanding and exceeding buyers' evolving expectations. Without embedding truly customer-centric mindsets, processes and technologies into the fabric of go-to-market strategies, it becomes almost impossible to consistently anticipate needs, nurture trust and expand value across dynamic customer lifecycles.

As markets face relentless upheaval, the bar for positive engagement only rises. Sales teams clinging to status quo playbooks rapidly lose relevance in the face of mounting complexity. On the other hand, leaders embracing frameworks to perpetually realign around customer requirements will sustain differentiation and growth regardless of external change and internal barriers.

Cultivating a Customer-Focused Culture

Transforming sales organizations into powerhouses of customer-centricity starts with nurturing employee mindsets, skills and behaviors completely focused on maximizing buyer success. Hire and develop professionals with equal parts empathy, curiosity and courage to challenge assumptions. Create psychologically safe environments encouraging candid insight sharing on improving experiences. Celebrate teams exhibiting creative passion for identifying unseen needs. Embed customer metrics into goal setting and rewards.

Continuously Gathering Crucial Context

Instilling cultural dedication to customers then equips salespeople to gather crucial contextual intelligence informing the next phase of transformation – realigning processes on buyer journeys versus internal functions. Implement mechanisms enabling large-scale voice-of-the-customer data assembly such as interviews, win/loss analysis, surveys and feedback communities. Feed insights into journey mapping workshops uncovering fluid experience gaps. Pressure test findings through observational field research. Commit to not just gathering feedback, but truly listening and understanding.

Innovating Holistic Solutions in Real-Time

Armed with actionable customer insights, organizations can then build capabilities delivering tailored solutions completely aligned to individual buyer requirements in-the-moment across channels. Invest in stacking advanced technologies like AI, predictive analytics and interaction adapters onto existing CRM and sales enablement platforms to sense signals and orchestrate hyper-personalization at scale. But also dedicate resources into building organizational dexterity responding to emerging needs with human nuance.

Continually Tracking and Improving Relevance

While many transformation efforts lose momentum over time, instilling an ethos of continual improvement sustains change and relevance even amidst volatility. Implement mechanisms to monitor engagement across channels, document competitive offerings and regularly reconnect with loyal customers and lost opportunities. Look for patterns pointing to universal experience gaps versus one-off cases. Be unafraid of major innovation cycles but also champion gradual, compounding enhancements.

The Bottom Line

In an era where customer allegiance constantly wavers, sales organizations require comprehensive frameworks nurturing enduring customer centricity and adaptability company-wide. The strategies and tools covered in this book provide roadmaps to launch this transformation, but real results stem from systemic commitment to keeping customers at the nucleus – not just during temporary campaigns, but through a paradigm cementing their ever-evolving reality into all priorities and processes forever.

www.ingramcontent.com/pod-product-compliance
Lightning Source LLC
Chambersburg PA
CBHW062339290526
45794CB00005B/2061